WRITERS AND THEIR WORK

ISOBEL ARMSTRONG
*General Editor*

# TED HUGHES

# TED HUGHES

## Susan Bassnett

To Luke, who writes and Rosie, who cares

© Copyright 2009 by Susan Bassnett

First published in 2009 by Northcote House Publishers Ltd, Horndon, Tavistock, Devon, PL19 9NQ, United Kingdom.
Tel: +44 (0) 1822 810066  Fax: +44 (0) 1822 810034.

**British Library Cataloguing-in-Publication Data**
A catalogue record for this book is available from the British Library

ISBN 978-0-7463-1061-8 hardcover
ISBN 978-0-7463-1003-8 paperback

Typeset by PDQ Typesetting, Newcastle-under-Lyme
Printed and bound in the United Kingdom

# Contents

# Acknowledgements

I am grateful to Isobel Armstrong for encouraging me to write this book, and to Brian Hulme for his patience. Daniel Weissbort has been an invaluable help, supplying me with rare copies of early numbers of *Modern Poetry in Translation*, sharing his inside knowledge of Ted Hughes's writing practice and acting as a critical friend throughout. My thanks, as ever, to Janet Bailey, whose secretarial skills are second to none, and to my daughter Rosanna for endless practical assistance. In the final stages of writing, I am grateful to Geoffrey for his unfailing love and support.

# Biographical Outline

1930    Born August 17 in Mytholmroyd, Yorkshire, to William
        Henry Hughes and Edith (*née* Farrar). Youngest child,
        brother Gerald ten years older, sister Olwyn two years
        older.
1937    Moves with family to Mexborough, South Yorkshire.
1943    Starts at Mexborough Grammar School where his
        interest in literature develops encouraged by John
        Fisher.
1948    Scholarship to Pembroke College, Cambridge.
1949    Starts two years National Service at Fylingdales.
1951    Goes up to Cambridge to read English.
1953    Changes to study archaeology and anthropology and
        has dream about the fox that inspired his first collection.
1954    Leaves Cambridge. Begins to publish poetry.
1955    Writes 'The Thought-Fox'.
1956    Meets and marries Sylvia Plath.
1957    *The Hawk in the Rain* is published to critical acclaim. Goes
        with Sylvia to teach on the East Coast of the United
        States.
1959    Travels with Sylvia around the US, spends two months
        at Yaddo Artists' Colony, then returns to England in
        December. His family are now living in Heptonstall,
        where they moved in 1952.
1960    Publishes *Lupercal* which wins Hawthornden Prize. *The
        Hawk in the Rain* wins Somerset Maugham Award.
        Hughes is now acclaimed as important young poet.
        Daughter Frieda born in April.
1961    Hughes and Plath move to Devon.
1962    Son Nicholas born. Falls in love with Assia Weevil and
        moves out of family home.

1963    Death of Sylvia Plath in February. Hughes left to bring up his small children. Publishes children's stories, *How the Whale Became* in November.

1965    Founds *Modern Poetry in Translation* with Daniel Weissbort. Editing Plath's last poems, helps to organize international poetry festival for Arts Council.

1966    Begins to work on Crow poems to go with drawings by Leonard Baskin.

1967    Daughter Alexandra Weevil (Shura) born. Publishes *Recklings* and *Wodwo*. Broadcasts *Poetry in the Making*.

1968    Publishes *The Iron Man*. His version of Seneca's *Oedipus* is performed. Continues to write Crow poems.

1969    Death of Assia and Shura. Death of his mother Edith. Publishes Seneca's *Oedipus* and introduction to poems of Vasco Popa.

1970    Publishes *The Coming of Kings* (four short plays), *Crow - From the Life and Songs of the Crow*. Marries Carol Orchard in August.

1971    Introduction and edition of *A Choice of Shakespeare's Verse*. Travels with Peter Brook to Persepolis to work on *Orghast*.

1972    Buys Moortown Farm in Devon and moves there with Carol and Jack Orchard, her father.

1973    Publishes *Orpheus* and *Prometheus on His Crag*.

1974    Publishes *Spring, Summer, Autumn, Winter*.

1975    Publishes *Season Songs*.

1976    Death of Jack Orchard. Publishes edition of selected poems of János Pilinszky.

1977    Publishes *Gaudete*. Awarded OBE.

1978    Publishes *Orts, Cave Birds, Moortown Elegies*.

1979    Publishes *Moon Bells, Remains of Elmet, Moortown, Adam and the Sacred Nine*.

1980    Goes fishing with son in Alaska, working on *River* poems.

1981    Publishes *Under the North Star* and *A Primer of Birds*.

1982    Edits *The Journals of Sylvia Plath*.

1983    Publishes *River*.

1984    Appointed Poet Laureate.

1985    Edits selected poems of Sylvia Plath.

1986    Publishes *Flowers and Insects*.

1987    Tribute to T.S. Eliot.

| | |
|---|---|
| 1988 | Publishes collection of fables, *Tales of the Early World*. |
| 1989 | Publishes *Moortown Diary* and *Wolfwatching*. |
| 1990 | Publishes *Capriccio*. |
| 1991 | Suffers from shingles, publishes very little. |
| 1992 | Publishes monograph, *Shakespeare and the Goddess of Complete Being*. Publishes *Rain Charm for the Duchy*. |
| 1993 | Publishes *The Iron Woman*. |
| 1994 | Publishes *Winter Pollen* and *Elmet*. |
| 1995 | Translating Aeschylus. His version of Wedekind's *Spring Awakening* is performed in London. *New Selected Poems* appears. |
| 1996 | His version of Lorca's *Blood Wedding* performed. Translating Ovid and Gawain poet. |
| 1997 | Publishes *Tales from Ovid*. Moortown Farm sold. |
| 1998 | Publishes *Birthday Letters*. *Tales from Ovid* awarded Whitbread Book of the Year Prize and W.H. Smith Literature Award. *Birthday Letters* wins Forward Prize for Poetry. His version of Racine's *Phèdre* performed starring Diana Rigg. Hughes appointed member of the Queen's Order of Merit. 28 October Ted Hughes dies. |
| 1999 | *The Oresteia* and *Alcestis* published. *Birthday Letters* wins T.S.Eliot Prize for Poetry, South Bank Award for Literature, the Whitbread Prize for Poetry and the Book of the Year prize. Memorial service for Hughes held in Westminster Abbey on 13 May. *The Oresteia* performed at the National Theatre. |

# Abbreviations

| | | |
|---|---|---|
| *BL* | *Birthday Letters* | Faber and Faber, 1998 |
| C | *Crow* | Faber and Faber, 1970 |
| *CP* | *Collected Poems* | Faber and Faber, 2003 |
| *HR* | *The Hawk in the Rain* | Faber and Faber, 1957 |

# Introduction

Those men and women born in Europe in the period between the two world wars perhaps saw the most radical changes of any generation alive in the twentieth century. Their parents could remember the world before the First World War, a world of clear class distinctions and relatively little social mobility, their children and grandchildren have grown up in completely different societies, and now inhabit the globalized world of the twenty-first century. Changes in life-style were revolutionary. Since the 1930s there have been valuable technological innovations that have followed one another with incredible rapidity – domestic electricity, radio, television, computers, the internet, all those mass communication systems that today we take for granted but which are relatively recent. Yet the twentieth century also saw genocide on an unprecedented scale, the invention of the atomic bomb, the Holocaust, the Cold War, the emergence of global terrorism and the breakdown of communities that had grown together over centuries. It is therefore unsurprising that a writer born at such a time should have returned again and again in his work to the theme of the eternal struggle between processes of often violent change and the stasis of changelessness. Nor is it surprising that the fortunes of any such writer should have fluctuated with the rapidly changing tastes of an uncertain age.

Ted Hughes was born in 1930, eleven years after the end of one world war and nine years before the start of the next. He came into the world in an England troubled by poverty and political divisiveness, into a community in rural Yorkshire where memories of the suffering endured by men in the trenches were very much alive, and his early poetry is full of references to stories that he must have heard recounted in his

1

childhood. His generation was touched by war through relationships with the survivors and the bereaved. In 'My Uncle's Wound' the poet tries to make contact with the old man through his stories: 'I scavenged for a memory, crumbs of rust or of bone', but his uncle has lost touch: 'He became quiet/With his memories'. (*CP* 100–1). The last lines move back into the speaker's consciousness, establishing a relationship between an old man's memories of war and a younger man's empathy with the natural environment that he nevertheless knows and loves, despite its pitiless harshness:

> But I know memory
> As I know the blood-crammed dried out rabbit-coloured
> Crumbs of soil that thicken this earth,
> Or the blinding of the sun, or the green wheat blades
> Sucking the crumbled soil
> Into their glistenings.

(CP 101)

Throughout Hughes's poetry run images of war and destruction, overt references to the First World War in many of his early poems and again in his later work, along with more general, universalized images of violence and brutality. These images are interconnected with striking, often savage images from the natural world, representations of animals and the elements, sometimes depicted realistically, sometimes symbolically. Childhood in Yorkshire in the 1930s provided the foundation for his unique poetic discourse, in which he combines stories he had heard as a boy with his own meticulous observations of nature and with the vast store of knowledge that he acquired through a lifetime of reading.

When Ted Hughes died on October 28 1998, he was probably at the height of his fame. Poet Laureate since 1984, in the 1990s his writing began to appeal to new audiences and the quality of his final works showed that he had moved into new poetic territory. *Tales from Ovid*, which appeared in 1997 won the W.H. Smith award and the Whitbread 1998 Book of the Year award. Just before his death, his last collection of poems, *Birthday Letters* won the Forward Prize for Poetry and went into the best-seller lists, becoming one of the highest selling hardback books on the British market of the day. In his obituary for *The Independent*, Boyd Tonkin wrote:

The damns burst and the clouds lifted. Hughes' final two volumes promptly walked off with every award they competed for... Hughes ended his career garlanded in glory.[1]

The acclaim accorded to Hughes's last two collections, in particular to *Birthday Letters* ensured his lasting reputation as one of the great English poets of the twentieth century, a reputation established many years earlier with the publication of his earliest volumes, *The Hawk in the Rain* (1957) and *Lupercal* (1960). Tonkin's metaphoric reference to dark clouds lifting and pent-up waters bursting through damns refers to some of the work produced in Hughes' middle period, when personal difficulties led to what has often been described as unevenness in his poetic productivity. Yet though some of his work received equivocal or even hostile responses, he continued to write steadily over many years. Throughout his life Hughes wrote in a variety of genres: he produced poetry and essays, edited and translated a great deal, wrote a long study of Shakespeare that was not received favourably by critics, and produced memorable books for children. Yet what he is principally remembered for are the collections that mark the beginning and end of his life as a poet, most especially for *The Hawk in the Rain* and *Birthday Letters*.

When *The Hawk in the Rain* first appeared in 1957, Edwin Muir called it a 'surprising' first book.[2] The physicality of Hughes's language, the power of his images and the disturbing depiction of nature as violent and pitiless was quite different from the dominant trend in English poetry in the 1950s, typified in the writing of Philip Larkin, towards a more restrained, genteel, detached and often ironic voice. The hawk in the title poem is a creature of elemental power:

> His wings hold all creation in a weightless quiet,
> Steady as a hallucination in the streaming air.

> (*HR* 11)

In this poem, as in many others, the I-speaker observes and records what he sees, not seeking to understand or empathize. The emotional power in the poem comes from the juxtapositioning of what is seen and what is happening to the speaker. 'I drown in the drumming ploughland' is the opening phrase of the poem, the idea of death entering at the outset. The hawk hovers over its prey, yet even the killer may find itself blown to destruction when it least expects to die. The strong, harsh rhythms disturb and resonate. Hughes wrote with a passion in his first collection of poems that would characterize all his later poetry. That same passion, though in a different kind of language is evident in his last works, both in the Ovid recreations and the poems in *Birthday Letters*.

If *The Hawk in the Rain was* seen as surprising, *Birthday Letters* created even greater shock waves. Written over a long period and finally brought together in a single volume, *Birthday Letters* is a sequence of poems about Hughes's relationship with his first wife, Sylvia Plath that echoes the genre of confessional poetry which she had so powerfully developed in her own work. For several decades, following Plath's suicide in 1963, Hughes was dogged by her spectre, as critics compared the two poets, often rating Plath more highly and Hughes was pilloried for his treatment of his wife and blamed for her death. *Birthday Letters* brought out into the public domain Hughes's perspective on the marriage and on Plath's suicide. The poems are autobiographical, tracing the story of the two poets from their first meeting to her death, but they can also be read as a kind of dialogue, for time and again Hughes picks up on an image in one of Plath's poems and speaks to it. *Birthday Letters* was so unexpected that when it was first published in 1998 Stephen Moss in *The Guardian* opened his review as follows:

> The 'literary scoop' of the decade, the century, the millennium. Take your pick. The publication of Ted Hughes's poems about his first wife, Sylvia Plath, has produced the kind of publicity money can't buy and led *The Times*, which has been serializing the poems, to declare that they 'confirm the Poet Laureate's place as one of the great figures in English literature'.[3]

This is journalistic hyperbole of course, but it gives a flavour of the reaction to the volume when it came out. Since Hughes had kept silent for so long, his decision to publish such intensely personal poems created genuine shock waves. The lyrical beauty of the poems, the sensitivity of Hughes's rereading of both his own memories and Plath's poetry gives the volume an elegiac quality. Underpinning it is a sense of sadness at the inevitability of the collision between two so powerful yet so

4

incompatible people. One poem, 'Your Paris', sums up the abyss that separated the lovers even as they started out on what was meant to be a lifetime together. 'Your Paris,' he writes, 'was American', whereas his Paris 'was only just not German.' Plath's idea of Paris was that of the imaginary Paris of the great American tradition, the City of Light that had harboured so many great writers from the New World. For Hughes, in contrast, Paris was a city associated with the war that had devastated Europe when he was still a schoolboy, a city occupied by the Nazis, and saved by the French Resistance. These two conceptions of the same place came from two different life-experiences, and represent two different histories and mythologies. *Birthday Letters* explores the fault lines that were always present in the marriage, and does so with an understanding that Hughes must have only gradually acquired over decades.

The Plath-Hughes marriage has been the subject of numerous books and even a Hollywood film. The two writers met as students at Cambridge and began an intense love affair, based not only on physical attraction but also on a shared passion for poetry. Writing in her diary when *The Hawk in the Rain* won the Harpers first publication prize, Plath summed up the hope and joy with which they embarked on their marriage and their intention to live a life of writing:

> I am so glad Ted is first. All my pat theories against marrying a writer dissolve with Ted: his rejections more than double my sorrow & his acceptances rejoice me more than mine...it is as if he were the perfect male counterpart to my own self: each of us giving the other an extension of the life we believe in living: never becoming slaves to routine, secure jobs, money: but writing constantly, walking the world with every pore open, & living with love and faith.[4]

The collapse of the marriage after the birth of their two children and Hughes's relationship with Assia Wevill drove Plath to take her own life in February 1963. Hughes later took on the task of editing her work, though was criticized for some of his decisions. As interest in Plath grew, becoming virtually an industry in itself, so opinions polarized either for or against Hughes. Plath's grave was defaced more than once and the name of Hughes scratched off it. From being seen as a poet in his own right, Hughes was seen by many now primarily as

Sylvia Plath's unfaithful husband. The shock of Plath's death and his responsibility for their children affected his writing, and when Assia Wevill killed herself and their daughter in 1969, the same year in which Hughes's mother also died, though he continued to write, he appeared to be seeking inspiration from different sources, from myth and folk-tales and from writers working in other languages. The pain and turmoil in his private life had an impact on his poetry, and his struggle can be discerned as we read his work chronologically.

Hughes's interest in poetry began in adolescence and was encouraged by his English master John Fisher, who published some of his early poems in the Mexborough Grammar School magazine. In an essay for aspiring young writers, 'Capturing Animals', Hughes writes about his earliest attempts at poetry, and suggests that capturing and collecting small animals and writing poems came from the same source:

> In a way, I suppose, I think of poems as a sort of animal. They have their own life, like animals, by which I mean that they seem quite separate from any person, even from their author, and nothing can be added to them or taken away without maiming and perhaps even killing them. And they have a certain wisdom. They know something special... something perhaps which we are very curious to learn. Maybe my concern has been to capture not animals particularly and not poems, but simply things which have a vivid life of their own, outside mine.[5]

The link between the natural world and writing poetry was therefore experienced at an early age, and is one of the keys to understanding Hughes's work. Even at his most anguished, the natural world served as a source of inspiration. Another key is also to be found in this essay, Hughes's belief in the metamorphic process of writing and the transformative power of poetry. He advises his would-be poets to imagine what they are writing, to turn themselves into what they are writing about, to transform themselves into a state where words start magically to shape themselves. The mystic, the shaman, the creator who experiences creativity through a physical transformation recurs through Hughes's writing and the magical quality of poetry is exemplified in the example he gives, of his poem 'The Thought-Fox', which emerged from a vision of a fox that came to him out of the snow one night.

In 1948 Hughes won an open exhibition to Pembroke College, Cambridge to read English. Before he could take up his scholarship, he had to undertake two years of national service, and was stationed at Fylingdales, an isolated radar station on the North Yorkshire moors, going up to Cambridge in 1951 at the age of twenty-one. His experience of English at Cambridge was not particularly rewarding, and he eventually dropped the subject in preference for archaeology and anthropology. That anthropological training would serve his poetry well later. He was interested in world religions, in shamanism, and in myth, being particularly influenced by the idea of the triple goddess of nature, a motif that recurs through Plath's poetry as well. After the tragic deaths of Assia and Shura, he turned increasingly to mythological themes, producing darker poetry that, apart from his collection *Crow* (1970), did not enjoy much success. However, his writing diversified as he experimented: a book for children, *The Iron Man* appeared in 1968, and in 1973 and 1974 he wrote *Season Songs*. Another volume of poetry for children, *What is Truth?* was published in 1984. He also began writing for the theatre, and in 1972 he collaborated with Peter Brook to create *Orghast at Persepolis*. This piece was devised through improvisation, and Hughes created an invented language for the actors, designed to be comprehended only through patterns of sound.

The collaboration with Brook reflects Hughes's internationalism, though he has frequently been seen as a very English poet, one who writes with great power about aspects of the English landscape. In his essay. 'Englands of the Mind', Seamus Heaney links Ted Hughes, Geoffrey Hill and Philip Larkin together, describing them as three quintessentially English poets. Of Hughes's England, Heaney writes:

> Hughes' is a primeval landscape where stones cry out and horizons endure, where the elements inhabit the mind with a religious force, where the pebble dreams 'it is the foetus of God', 'where the staring angels go through', 'where all the stars bow down', where, with appropriately pre-Socratic force, water 'lies at the bottom of all things/utterly worn out utterly clear.' It is England as King Lear's heath which now becomes a Yorkshire moor where sheep and foxes and hawks persuade 'unaccommodated man' that he is a poor bare forked thing, kinned not in a chain but on a plane of being with the animals themselves. There monoliths and lintels. The air is menaced

by God's voice in the wind, by demonic protean crow-shapes; and the poet is a wanderer among the ruins, cut off by catastrophe from consolation and philosophy.[6]

Heaney rightly draws attention to Hughes's wild, northern landscapes and to what he describes as Hughes's attempts 'to make vocal the inner life, the simple beingthereness'. He points out Hughes's preoccupation with ritual, arguing that his is a sensibility that is fundamentally pagan, not in any way a sensibility of the city dweller. The Yorkshire landscape of his childhood recurs time and again in Hughes's poetry, along with the moorlands of Devon where he spent most of his adult life. His England is a place inhabited by foxes, hawks, otters and pikes, a place where birds plummet out of the sky to seize their prey, where cows, sheep and pigs are born, give birth in turn and die, locked in a strangely close yet utterly detached relationship with human beings. In a poem from *Moortown Diary* (1979) 'Ravens', the poet describes a newly-born lamb being torn to pieces by ravens – 'Its insides, the various jellies and crimsons and transparencies/ And threads and tissues pulled out/ In straight lines, like tent ropes'. The lamb has failed to survive and is providing sustenance for the birds; this is an inevitable fact of nature, where one creature feeds off another. But the speaker has a small child with him, who asks just one question: whether the lamb cried at birth. Three times the question is repeated, and the consolatory answer is yes, but the poem's focus on the physical detail of the lamb's corpse highlights the savagery of the natural world, beyond man's intervention and man's pity.

Despite the fundamental importance of the English land-scape and its inhabitants in Hughes's poetry, he should be regarded as a writer whose sources were both parochially English and international. From 1966 to 1971 he and another poet, Daniel Weissbort coedited *Modern Poetry in Translation* the journal that more than any other brought foreign poets to English-speaking readers. Weissbort remained a close friend and collaborator, and in 2002 published a collection entitled *Letters to Ted*. One poem, 'Not Saint Botolph's: An Antidote' recalls how the idea for the journal came from Hughes, and Weissbort speculates that founding it may have helped Hughes to start writing again after his wife's death:

8

Thirty-six years have passed but the magazine remained your protégé. It joined us in an enterprise that maybe got you going again – after Sylvia.[7]

Hughes worked with János Csokits on a volume of translations of poetry by the Hungarian János Pilinszky in 1976 and two years later wrote an introduction to a translation of the poetry of the Yugoslav poet Vasco Popa. In an essay on Hughes and eastern European poets, Michael Parker sees these writers, along with Zbigniew Herbert from Poland and Miroslav Holub from Czechoslovakia as exerting a profound influence on Hughes's writing. Parker notes the central significance of war in Hughes's consciousness, and suggests that these and other eastern European poets offered models of survival despite the bleakest horrors of occupation, death camps and genocide, providing a vital stimulus to a man reeling from the shock of his wife's suicide:

> The brave experimentation, the drive towards an ur-language, and above all the compassion and humility which pervade the writing of Herbert, Holub, Pilinszky and Popa helped Hughes to lift himself out of the abyss into which he has been hurled.[8]

The influence of these writers is evident in *Crow* (1970) and it is clear that from this time onwards, Hughes not only read a great deal of poetry translated from other languages, (the only language he had of speaking competence was French), but also undertook a significant number of translations, including Wedekind's *Spring Awakening* , *The Oresteia, Alcestis, Sir Gawain and the Green Knight,* Racine's *Phedre,* Lorca's *Blood Wedding,* work by Yehuda Amichai, in collaboration with Weissbort who also provided him with a first version of Pushkin's 'The Prophet'. His best-known translation is his version of selected tales from Ovid's *Metamorphoses.* He translated from contemporary writers and from great classical poets, creating both plays and new poetry in English, opening himself to a vast range of different sources.

What was central to Hughes's development as a poet was finding the right language. In one of his rare interviews, he talks about his search for his own language, pointing out that because of his childhood in Yorkshire, using the local dialect, he grew up with two languages in his head, what he calls a mother tongue

9

and a childhood tongue. He recognizes that he can no longer speak in the dialect of West Yorkshire, but says that this is what he hears when writing. The rhythms of his childhood language retain their power:

> And, maybe because it has disappeared and maybe because it isn't the language of English culture, maybe it's enabled me to keep hold of what was associated with it in the beginning. My first language had been ordinary English then the language would have been wide open and permeable by all the later added cultural influences and those first things – that I can hang onto, and make something of in verse – would have been enormously overlaid and evolved and so on.[9]

Ted Hughes died of a heart attack on 28 October 1998. He was already in hospital, receiving treatment for cancer. The obituarists hailed him as one of the great English poets, a poet who had also established himself as a great European writer. The success of his last two published collections appeared particularly ironic. Of Hughes it can indeed be said that he died at the height of his creative powers.

Ted Hughes was not only a great poet, he was a self-reflecting poet who sought to understand the complexities of the creative process. His essays on the work of other poets shed light on his own writing, and one of his most revealing essays is a study of how Sylvia Plath had come to write one of her poems. 'The Evolution of "Sheep in Fog"' is a study of one poet's drafts, which Hughes argues show the different stages of a phenomenon that only poets can recognize through their experience of it. At the moment of writing, he claims, four things can happen. The first of the four is when 'inspiration' takes over and the poem seems to write itself, 'finding its own perfect words, images, rhythms and shape'.[10] The example he cites here is Coleridge's 'Kubla Khan', and he points out that this experience is very rare. The second is what happens when the poem half-emerges. Here the metaphor he uses is of the poet as midwife, struggling to assist at a birth. As the poet struggles, so the risk is that the poem may be damaged or even destroyed. The task of the poet is to be submissive and trust in the process itself. T.S.Eliot's *The Waste Land* is cited as an example of what can happen when a poet lets go and allows a poem to emerge spontaneously, 'complete and ready made from nowhere'. The third way of making a poem is that which, according to Hughes, accounts for most of the poetry ever written, for here what happens is that inspiration fuses with techniques learned by writing and reading other poetry. Hughes, like Plath, believed that poetry was both an art and a craft, and that poets had to keep honing their skills and never relaxing their disciplined approach to their work. That constant vigilance and sheer hard work is exhausting and can be full of conflict, hence the fourth kind of poem, which he terms a more interesting variant of the third, is one that comes out of the poet's efforts to create. The imagery Hughes uses is bellicose – the poem is 'a sort of hard-fought treaty', it is a kind of reconciliation, 'a precarious, jagged, touchy kind of agreement'. Such poems can be exciting even when not perfect. He goes on to examine the drafts of 'Sheep in Fog', showing how they demonstrate in some way something of all these four procedures. Hughes's own drafts have been studied likewise, and the drafting stages provide insights into how a poem comes into being, from inside the poet's head and onto the printed page.

It is impossible to do justice to the size and complexity of Hughes's writing in a single small volume. Hughes was not only a poet who was honoured finally as Poet Laureate, he was also a children's author, a Shakespeare scholar, a playwright, an essayist and broadcaster, an inspirational teacher of writing, the inventor of a new dramatic language and a translator. This book will therefore necessarily be a selective, partial analysis of his writing, a sketch broadly delineating principal lines that run through his poetry like geological strata . It is organized roughly chronologically, in five chapters, each of which focuses on a particular strand in Hughes's work. Chapter 1 is concerned with Hughes as a nature poet, and examines the ways in which his writing about the natural world evolved from his first collection, *The Hawk in the Rain* to *River* that appeared over a quarter of a century later. Chapter 2 examines the idea of the poet as shaman and focuses on the controversial Crow poems, which led some critics, wrongly, to think of Hughes as a poet who celebrated violence. The nightmare vision of Crow, however, marks a stage in Hughes's evolution as a poet, and in chapter 3 the importance of history is discussed. Hughes kept exploring his English roots, writing about the durability of language, the relationship between past and present in terms of both people and landscape, and about his own immediate family. In chapter 4, Hughes's use of two fundamental myths that connect all his writing is analysed. The Great Goddess and the figure of Prometheus recur time and again in his work, explicitly and implicitly, and through these myths he developed his theories of poetic language. Finally, chapter 5 argues that Hughes was a great translator, in the broadest sense of that term. Hughes had promoted translation through his editing of *MPT* in the 1960s, and his interest in translation not only endured, but increased in his latter years, his final works all being, in one way or another forms of translation.

# 1

## 'A sudden sharp hot stink of fox': Ted Hughes and Nature

In an interview in the *London Magazine* in January 1971, Hughes spoke about the impact of his birthplace on his language. Pointing out that he grew up in West Yorkshire, where a very distinctive dialect is spoken, he went on to suggest that one's childhood dialect stays alive in some way, 'in a sort of inner freedom'. Without his own particular form of speech, he feels he would never have been able to write poetry, adding that West Yorkshire dialect is directly connected to Middle English.[1] This historical connection was to lead him later to translate one of the greatest Middle English poems, *Sir Gawain and the Green Knight* and to write a version of a Greek tragedy for Northern Broadsides, a theatre company that performs classic works in Northern dialect. The rhythms of West Yorkshire speech with its strong oral dialect tradition gave him the impetus to write and sustained him in his writing throughout his life.

Hughes was always preoccupied with patterns of sound. In his first collection, *The Hawk in the Rain*, his bold use of alliteration, assonance, consonant clusters and compound words gives a physicality to a variety of subjects. In 'The Martyrdom of Bishop Farrar', the burning is depicted by piling words on words:

> The sullen-jowled watching Welsh townspeople
> Hear him crack in the fire's mouth; they see what
> Black oozing twist of stuff bubbles the smell
> That tars and retches their lungs

> (*HR* 61)

The desperate running of a caged wild animal in a zoo in 'The Jaguar' is portrayed through the repetitive use of b and s sounds:

> The eye satisfied to be blind in fire,
> By the bang of the blood in the brain deaf the ear –
> He spins from the bars, but there's no cage to him
>
> More than to the visionary his cell:
> His stride is the wildernesses of freedom:

(HR 12)

In 'Fallgrief's Girl-Friends' the man speaks in recognizable Yorkshire:

> While I am this muck of man in this
> Muck of existence, I shall not seek more
> Than a muck of a woman

(HR 29)

*The Hawk in the Rain* is a collection of diverse poems that clearly show a poet playing with language, shaping it like clay, and drawing upon different linguistic varieties – Anglo-Saxon and Middle English, the language of the King James Bible, the language of great English poets of the past, Shakespeare and Wordsworth and Gerard Manley Hopkins and the oral varieties of language with which he had grown up. Seamus Heaney sees the richness of his language figuratively, in terms of the history of a very masculine England:

> His consonants are the Norsemen, the Normans, the Roundheads in the world of his vocables, hacking and hedging and hammering down the abundance and luxury and possible lasciviousness of his vowels.[2]

There is a speakability that runs through poem after poem, an early indication of Hughes' talent for writing for the theatre that would emerge in due course. In 'The Horses' the moment when the sun breaks through early morning moorland mist is described in a rolling wave of words, connected by complex sonorous echoes:

> Slow detail leafed from the darkness. Then the sun
> Orange, red, red erupted
>
> Silently, and splitting to its core tore and flung cloud,

14

Shook the gulf open, showed blue,

And the big planets hanging –

(HR 16)

Hughes's innovative use of language was combined with a startling ability to write about the natural world, in particular about the animal kingdom. Talking about his writing, he acknowledged an interest in animals that, he said, 'began when I began', and explained how in his middle teens he started to look more closely at animals, trying to see in his imagination from their point of view.[3] In *The Hawk in the Rain* animals include the hawk, a jaguar, a macaw, horses, wolves and the creature that recurs throughout his writing, the fox. The most famous poem in this collection, and probably the most anthologised of all Hughes's poetry is 'The Thought-Fox'.

Discussing this poem, Hughes pointed out that the thought-fox is both a real fox and yet not real. It is an imaginary creature that has all the characteristics of the real animal, yet does not actually materialize. The poem begins with the poet sitting late at night at a desk, imagining a forest somewhere. His pages are blank, outside the window he cannot see any stars, inspiration is not coming to him. Into this lonely, desolate state comes a creature, that gradually begins to take shape: first its nose, then its eyes, then its pawprints in the snow, then its 'lame shadow', the sign 'of a body that is bold to come'. The thought-fox crosses clearings, moves between the trees, coming closer, going 'about its own business'. Then in the final stanza, the fox and the writer are joined:

> Till, with a sudden sharp hot stink of fox
> It enters the dark hole of the head.
> The window is starless still; the clock ticks,
> The page is printed.

(HR 15)

The thought-fox is the symbol of poetic inspiration; a creation in the mind of the writer, it acquires a life of its own then metaphorically enters the man's head. The fox for Hughes is his totemic animal, and just as creators and shamans in primitive societies dress in the skins of totemic animals, so he equates his ability to create poetry with an almost mystical union with a fox.

15

In 'Foxhunt', one of the poems in *Moortown* (1979) the moment when hounds pick up a fox's scent is depicted first through the sounds of the chase – 'the idiot pack-noise, the puppyish whine-yelps', then through the reactions of other creatures such as crows and blackbirds to the noise. The survival of the fox hangs in the balance:

> Will he run
> Till his muscles suddenly turn to iron,
> Till blood froths his mouth as his lungs tatter,
> Till his feet are raw blood-sticks and his tail
> Trails thin as a rat's? Or will he
> Make a mistake, jump the wrong way, jump right
> Into the hound's mouth?

*(CP 507)*

There is no way of answering these questions, but there is hope. The concluding words of the poem depict the writer writing and the fox still running, still with a chance of survival:

> As I write this down
> He runs still fresh, with all his chances before him.

*(CP 507)*

*Moortown* reflects a happier period in Hughes's life, following his marriage to Carol Orchard in 1970 and his purchase of Moortown Farm in Devon in 1972. Just as the fox stands a chance of escaping the hounds, so Hughes the man stands a chance of escaping from the furies that have pursued him in the recent past. The violence of the animal kingdom and the inexorability of death are still strongly present in this collection, but there is a more hopeful note, as reflected in ' Foxhunt' and the fox may live to be chased another day.

The central significance of the fox returns in Hughes's last collection, *Birthday Letters*. 'Epiphany' tells how the poet was walking over Chalk Farm Bridge in London when a man tried to sell him a fox cub he was carrying under his coat. The poem charts the poet's astonishment, the conversation with the man who offers the cub for a pound, then the rapid calculations as to how a fox might fit into a small flat with a baby. The needs of the fox are beautifully sketched:

What would we do with an unpredictable
Powerful, bounding fox?
The long-mouthed, flashing temperament?
That necessary nightly twenty miles
And that vast hunger for everything beyond us?

(*BL* 114)

The little fox and the poet gaze at one another, and then the man walks on. Years later, writing this poem , he returns to that fox cub with new insight. If he had bought it, if he had paid the pound and taken the fox back home, if he had 'grasped that whatever comes with a fox/Is what tests a marriage and proves it a marriage', if he had understood the symbolic significance of what that fox represented

I would not have failed the test. Would you have failed it?
But I failed. Our marriage had failed.

(*BL* 115)

Just as the fox is the creature that provides him with the creative energy to begin writing poetry, so the fox is the animal that enables him to see when and how his marriage to Sylvia Plath had failed. The clash between the compromises demanded by marriage and the domestic world and the vastness of what Hughes describes as the 'huge whisper of the constellations' is too great. Keith Sagar, writing about this poem summarizes beautifully what the fox signified to Hughes in his life:

He identifies the fox with his own inner meaning, his authenticity, the ultimate truth of his being, the god or luminous spirit in him, the *nagual*, the *duende*.

That inner authenticity has been compromised and the incompatibility of the two poets, whose marriage had begun so well and with so much promise is now exposed. Once again a fox has shown Hughes his inner self.

Three years after the award-winning *The Hawk in the Rain* appeared, Hughes published *Lupercal*. Animals abound in this collection also: wolves, foxes, horses, an old tomcat, the bull Moses, a dead pig, an otter, a bullfrog, a pike and several birds, including hawks, crows and thrushes. The poem simply entitled 'Thrushes' is one of the most powerful. Here thrushes on the lawn are depicted as killing machines, programmed to 'bounce and stab'. The second stanza questions what this programming might be – 'Mozart's brain had it, and the shark's mouth'. Creative genius can also be destructive, though both the shark and the thrush kill in order to eat. The final stanza compares this savage animal existence with that of man, sitting at a desk, or carving tiny ornaments or performing 'heroisms on horseback'. Yet even while he is engaged in some activity or another, all around him are 'furious spaces of fire', and a 'wilderness of black silent waters'. Man can only try to stay in control of his own life; how pathetic that endeavour is can be seen in the contrast between the third stanza and the first, where the birds are introduced:

> Terrifying are the attent sleek thrushes on the lawn,
> More coiled steel than living

> (CP 82)

A similar message is to be found in 'Hawk Roosting', where the speaker is the bird himself:

> I kill where I please because it is all mine.
> There is no sophistry in my body:
> My manners are tearing off heads –

> (CP 69)

In an interview, Hughes claimed that what he was trying to do with the hawk poem was to write about Nature, about Nature actually thinking through the mind of the bird.[4] Nature is merciless and unchanging – 'Nothing has changed since I began' – nor is any change to the order of things possible. The final line of the poem insists on the unvarying repetition of a natural order that has always existed and that is outside any man-made moral universe: 'I am going to keep things like this.'

Closely related to 'Hawk Roosting' is 'Pike'. Hughes had a passion for fishing that had begun in his boyhood, and in this poem he recalls a favourite fishing place. The pike, like the hawk is a natural-born killer – pike are 'killers from the egg', with fangs 'not to be changed at this date'. They hover in dark waters, beneath lily pads waiting to strike. The poet recalls how he took three small pike home and kept them in a tank, and how they devoured one another until only the most effective killer was left. These childhood memories are given a wider dimension as the fishpond is described as 'deep as England'. Beneath the supposedly calm surface, death waits, and the implication is that darker forces lurk beneath the veneer of civilization.

What is striking about the poems in *Lupercal* is their strong pictorial quality. The Anglo-Saxon heaviness of the language of *The Hawk in the Rain* is much less evident, and though the images of Nature's unbending savagery are disturbing, the balance between sound and image is more elegantly maintained. What can be seen very plainly is the almost photographic quality of much of the descriptive language. The otter, 'an eels'/Oil of water body' has 'webbed feet and a long ruddering tail/And a round head like an old tomcat' ('The Otter'), an old cat's eyes open in twilight 'green as ringstones: he yawns wide red/Fangs as a lady's needle and bright' ('Esther's Tomcat'). Some of the most beautiful poems are about northern landscapes. 'Mayday on Holderness' offers a panoramic view of Yorkshire stretching out to the sea:

> From Hull's sunset smudge
> Humber is melting eastward, my south skyline:
> A loaded single vein, it drains
> The effort of the inert North – Sheffield's ores,
> Bog pools, dregs of toadstools, tributary
> Graves, dunghills, kitchens, hospitals.
> The unkillable North Sea swallows it all.
> Insects, drunken, drop out of the air.

> (*CP* 60)

The vastness of the landscape takes the poet outwards, on a Wordsworthian journey into the metaphysical. The world of insects, animals and birds are summoned as the message of the inexorability of life and death is expressed: 'Dead and unborn are in God comfortable'. The world of human history is also present, through references to the instruments of war, to bombs and bayonets and an overt reference to Gallipoli. Hughes's father William had been one of only seventeen young men from a regiment of the Lancashire Fusiliers killed at Gallipoli who had survived, and his father's experience of the war had a powerful impact on the young Hughes. Several critics have noted the confluence of images of war and images from the natural world that seem to underpin Hughes's poetry, and this poem is a good example of that fusion of thought-paths.

19

'Pennines in April' is another poem that follows a similar pictorial pattern: a great roving cinematic opening, as the poet's eye spans the horizon, then a shift into another dimension. In this poem, the Pennines themselves seem alive and in motion as the eye scans slowly over the 'miles of silence':

> Landscapes gliding blue as water
> Those barrellings of strength are heaving slowly and heave
> To your feet and surf upwards
> In a still, fiery air, hauling the imagination,
> Carrying the larks upwards.

(*CP* 68)

The hills are an elemental force, they drag the imagination upwards in some primeval energetic surge. Just as Hughes writes about animals and from within the mind of animals, so he also anthropomorphizes the land itself in this poem. The fox enters the poet's head and sparks his creative imagination, the land surges beneath him like a sea, stones and soil in motion to propel the mind upwards.

When *Lupercal* was published in 1960 Hughes was already writing poems that would appear in his next collection, *Wodwo* (1967). Those seven years were critical ones; Sylvia Plath took her own life in 1963, and Hughes had embarked on a different pattern of writing, producing books for children, translating and reading extensively in folklore and anthropology. The same attention to detail in natural description is still there in the *Wodwo* poems, but there are other, new elements that derive from very different sources from those which inspired the earlier works. Hughes himself wrote that poetry comes out of particular, individual experiences undergone by the poet, experiences that 'because of something in their nature, keep[s] happening to them again and again.'[5] Experiences can be narrow, such as the epiphanic moments experienced by Wordsworth, or very varied, though Hughes is of the view that the wider the poet's experience, the greater the potential of the poetry. It was the breadth of experience that drew him to the work of Eastern European poets, experiences of extreme suffering and survival. Michael Parker sees the influence of some of the poets discovered by Hughes in the 1960s echoed in his writing:

In their exposure of the blackest, innermost recesses of Man's being and their questioning of the entire metaphysical structure of the universe which appears to ordain endless, purposeless suffering, and in the startling directness with which the most horrific experiences are confronted, Hughes' poems in *Wodwo* and *Crow*, owe much, therefore, to the eastern European revelation.[6]

Parker suggests that 'Skylarks', one of the first poems written by Hughes after a period of silence, is underpinned by the idea of suicide as the price to be paid for the gift of poetry, a theme deriving both from Plath and from Vasko Popa. The skylark flies singing because it cannot do anything else, sings itself to exhaustion, then falls back to the earth. The watching poet is appalled, seeing the bird in its 'nightmare difficulty', thrashing its feathers, struggling to fulfil its destiny. The simple, observed scene takes on a dark, symbolic dimension.

A first version of this poem appeared in *Wodwo* (1967). Two further sections (nos. 4 and 8) were added later when Hughes revised the poem, as he did with so much of his work. Rewriting and reshaping his poetry, in the way a master craftsman will return to tinker with work he deems not to be quite as he would have wished it, implies that Hughes had a strong sense of self-awareness and a lack of arrogance. Time and again he points out what he perceived as the failings of something he had written, how he had not quite achieved what he wanted, refusing to see art as definitive. Writing about T.S Eliot, Hughes commented:

> The poet's each successive creation can be read as the poetic self's effort to make itself known, to further its takeover...successive visions evolve in time according to the way the poetic self evolves in its hidden life.[7]

The poetic self is in a constant state of evolution, hence the impossibility of ever creating a definitive, completely finished work.

'Skylarks' is, in one respect, a poem about the evolution of the poetic self. In the first section of the poem, the skylark flies upwards. The opening line is a statement, 'The lark begins to go up', but immediately there is a sombre note; the bird is rising 'like a warning'. The skylark is compared to an Indian of the high Andes, its 'whippet head, barbed like a hunting arrow'. But its flight is not effortless; three times the word 'leaden' is repeated, and the flight of the skylark is seen as part of a struggle against life forces and the potential for self-destruction. The second section describes the lark as 'crueller than owl or eagle', cruel because the bird is obeying its natural imperative to climb and to sing, which is its reason for being, oblivious as to why it is programmed to behave in this way. The poet then addresses the bird directly in the third section, in lines that contrast the creation of poetry with the bird's capacity to create song:

> I suppose you just gape and let your gaspings
> Rip in and out through your voicebox
> > O lark
> And sing inwards as well as outwards
> Like a breaker of ocean milling the shingle
> > O lark
> O song, incomprehensibly both ways
> Joy! Help! Joy! Help!
> > O lark

> > > > (CP 173–4)

Here the connection with one of the great Romantic poems becomes evident. Shelley's ode 'To a Skylark' is a hymn of praise to the bird whose capacity to touch the realms of joy are envied by the earthbound poet. The first verse is one of the most famous verses in English literature:

> Hail to thee, blithe Spirit!
> Bird thou never wert,
> That from Heaven, or near it
> Pourest thy full heart
> In profuse strains of unpremeditated art.

Shelley's skylark embodies the ecstasy of creation, producing pure, perfect art that rises beyond the human. Hughes's skylark, in contrast, sings because it is programmed to sing, it is destined to sing until sucked dry by an uncaring sun. The birds' singing goes on and on, the larks 'carry their tongues to the last atom', exhausting themselves in a frenzy of music. The destructive impulse inherent in the creating of art is all too clear: poets and skylarks alike are doomed to create and be damaged in the process, but they cannot resist the impulse that drives them both in their different ways to sing. In the eighth section, added later, the focus shifts from the poet watching the bird fly up and plunge back to earth again, exhausted, to a mythical figure, Cuchulain, bound in torment to a pillar, listening to the 'blind song' of the lark. This is an interesting addition, and though it alters the balance of the poem, it introduces an element that connects poetry to myth and story-telling, something that was increasingly happening in Hughes's work more generally.

*Wodwo* has never been seen as one of Hughes's best collections, but it is important in several ways: it reflects a widening out both thematically and formally from his previous writing, and the poet's struggle with himself and with his material is apparent. Alongside poems there are stories and a play, so that the collection is more varied than his previous books. The title is significant: it derives from Middle English, and the volume is prefaced by four lines from *Sir Gawain and the Green Knight*:

> Sometimes with dragons he wars, and with wolves also,
> Sometimes with wild men of the woods (*wodwos*) who lived
> among the crags,
> Both with bulls and bears, and boars at other times
> And giants that pursued him over the high fell.

> (*CP* 146)

The poet equates himself with the wodwo, the wild man of the woods. The prose-poem 'Wodwo' is a monologue, beginning with the three word question 'What am I?' There is little punctuation, save question marks and as the wodwo questions who and what he is, he tries to understand what place he might have in the world and how he may have come into being:

> I seem
> Separate from the ground and not rooted but dropped
> out of nothing casually I've no threads
> fastening me to anything I can go anywhere
> I seem to have been given the freedom
> of this place what am I then?

> (*CP* 183)

Although the word 'freedom' is rarely used, it is a keyword in *Wodwo*. 'Wings' is a poem in three parts, the first of which is entitled 'M. Sartre considers current affairs'. The connection between Sartre's existentialist philosophy, with his statement that the absolute freedom of the human being is terrible and the desolation of the wild man of the woods is obvious. Freedom, in Sartre's universe leads to destruction. Hughes was wrestling with similar thoughts. Keith Sagar points out that the two 'most up-beat' poems 'Wodwo' and 'Full Moon and Little Frieda' were placed deliberately at the end of the book, and adds that both were written before Plath's death. However, despite this attempt at a slightly less dark ending, Sagar is in no doubt that *Wodwo* and *Recklings,* that was also published in 1967, are despairing works:

> We are in a wasteland, a dark intestine, pointless cycle of recurrence, a dark night of the soul, a world very like that of Samuel Beckett.[8]

In 'A Wind Flashes the Grass' the savagery of the weather, the hostility of the landscape, the whole destructive force of nature terrify and astound. There is no I-speaker in this poem, instead, unusually, there is the plural 'we', introduced in the first two lines:

> Leaves pour blackly across.
> We cling to the earth, with glistening eyes, pierced afresh
> > By the trees' cry.
>
> > > (*CP* 153)

We, that is humanity, can only cling on as the storm rages, a storm reminiscent of *The Inferno*, for as Dante descends into Hell he encounters the circle of doomed lovers, blown forever like leaves by a black wind. We are compelled to listen, 'for below words/ Meanings that will not part from the rock'. The poem moves to focus on a ploughman, suddenly becoming anxious, who is transformed in the hellish wind into something other-worldly as his normality disintegrates – 'his tractor becomes terrible' – and 'the shadow of his bones tosses darkly on the air.'

The bleakness of much of the writing of this period of Hughes's life is clear to see, but as will be discussed later when we consider the Crow poems, there was also a strain of dark humour and, perhaps because he struggled so successfully to survive by confronting his daemons, he also found a way to a more life-centring poetry. Hughes was a caring father whose devotion to his children can be seen in the poems and stories he wrote for his daughter Frieda and son Nicholas, and in the way in which he guarded the privacy of his family. *Season Songs* (1976) is a collection of poems for children, and began as a pamphlet published in 1968 for performance by schoolchildren in Little Missenden. A later edition in 1985 modified the collection again, adding some poems and removing others. These are poems which reflect Hughes's extraordinary ability to observe natural phenomena and to make connections that would appeal to children and adults alike. His daffodils are like soldiers:

> A spurt of daffodils, stiff, quivering –
> Plumes, blades, creases, Guardsmen
> At attention ('Spring Nature Notes')

(CP 310)

Fledglings struggle to learn to fly:

> Every year a first-fling, nearly flying
> Misfit flopped in our yard,
> Groggily somersaulting to get airborne. ('Swifts')

(CP 315)

The new-born lamb has a 'stubby/White wool pyramid head on a tottery neck' ('Sheep'), while in autumn 'The chestnut splits its padded cell/It opens an African eye' ('Autumn Nature Notes'). In 'Hay', the wind blows across the grass, only this time

> The grass is happy
> To run like a sea, to be glossed like a mink's fur
> By polishing wind.

(CP 317)

Hughes wrote a version of 'Who killed Cock Robin?' mourning the death of leaves in autumn. The apple claims to have killed the leaves, then all of nature joins in the mourning process, the crow as the parson, the river digging the grave, the sunset carrying the coffin and finally the robin tolling the bell. Though there is sadness here, it is an elegiac sadness, and the bleakness has gone.

One of the most beautiful poems in this collection is 'The Warm and the Cold' in which the ways in which creatures survive the harshness of winter is depicted through a series of images. Hughes uses rhyme and repetition in this poem very precisely, and the duality of warmth and coldness is perfectly balanced. The first stanza strings a set of comparative pictures together to contrast with the harshness of winter, described as a steel trap, and the stanza hinges, as do the other two stanzas, on the crucial word 'but':

> Freezing dusk is closing
> Like a slow trap of steel
> On trees and roads and hills and all
> That can no longer feel.
> But the carp is in its depth
> Like a planet in its heaven
> And the badger in its bedding
> Like a loaf in the oven.
> And the butterfly in its mummy
> Like a viol in its case.
> And the owl in its feathers
> Like a doll in its lace.

(CP 343)

In 1979 Hughes published *Moortown*, a collection that included three works already in print, though in small runs, with Rainbow Press (*Prometheus on His Crag; Moortown Elegies; Adam and the Sacred Nine*) along with a fourth section, *Earth-numb*. Later, in 1989, Hughes dismantled this arrangement and brought out *Moortown Diaries* as a separate volume, which he dedicated to the memory of his father-in-law, Jack Orchard, of whom he had been extremely fond and who had died in 1976. In his preface to the 1989 edition, Hughes explains how he came to write these poems:

> The pieces in this collection came about by the way. It occurred to me from time to time that interesting things were happening, and that I ought to make a note of them, a note of the details in particular, partly with the idea of maybe using them at some future time in a piece of writing, and partly to make a fleeting snapshot, for myself of a precious bit of my life. Over those first years, as the evidence now shows me, that impulse came to me about forty times.[9]

Hughes goes on to explain that he wrote in verse because it was the easiest way for him to make notes based on close observation. Shaping the notes into lines, he says, made the recording process easier. The improvised verses were therefore a way of focusing his attention on the detail and excluding anything that might not be relevant. He explains that this way of writing was effectively a memory-shaping process; it needed to be done quickly, as soon after the scene that he wanted to

26

record had taken place, since to wait meant that what he calls new patterns resulting from memory began to take over. Later, when asked to give an editor some poems, he went back to these verse-notes and looked again, starting with 'February 17th':

> It didn't take me long to realize I was in the position of a translator: whatever I might make of the passage, I was going to have to destroy the original. And what was original here was not some stranger's poem but the video and surviving voice-track of one of my own days, a moment of my life that I did not want to lose.[10]

Significantly, Hughes refers to himself as a translator here, equating the creative process with translation. *Moortown* shows Hughes in touch with his roots as a countryman. The remorselessness of the cycle of life and death is at the heart of the poems, but what we have here is a poetry that is grounded in experience, and symbolic struggles with the elements take second place. Hughes had gone to live on a farm on the edge of Dartmoor in Devon, with his wife Carol and her father, where he raised sheep and cattle. A powerful central theme in the collection is the difficulty and dangers of the lambing and calving season. 'February 17th' opens with a blunt statement of fact: 'A lamb could not get born'. The poet tries to help the birthing sheep, but cannot. The lamb's head has slipped out too soon, there is no way that the ewe can push the rest of its body out. What follows is an almost scientific account of what a farmer has to do in such circumstances: first he tries to pull the lamb out with a rope, then when this fails

> I went
> Two miles for the injection and a razor.
> Sliced the lamb's throat-strings, levered with a knife
> Between the vertebrae and brought the head off

> (*CP* 519)

Having saved the ewe, he struggles to help her push out the remains of the lamb

> Till it came.
> And after it the long, sudden, yolk-yellow
> Parcel of life
> In a smoking slither of oils and soups and syrups –
> And the body lay born, beside the hacked-off head.

> (*CP* 519)

In farming, as these poems remind us, the needs of the living always take precedence, and there can be no sentimentality at such times. Yet the poet also acknowledges the animal power of motherhood. In 'Last Night' a ewe will not leave her dead twin lambs, in 'Struggle' a cow feeds her feeble calf, losing the fight for life, in 'Happy Calf' the cow is humanized, unusually for Hughes – 'Mother is worried, her low, short moos/Question what's going on.' In 'Sheep', the bleating of ewes is compared symbolically to the mourning of mothers in wartime:

> The mothers have come back
> From the shearing, and behind the hedge
> The woe of sheep is like a battlefield
> In the evening, when the fighting is over,
> And the cold begins, and the dew falls,
> And bowed women move with water.

> > (CP 532)

There is a sacramental quality to Hughes's writing in these poems. Previously, he had offered readers a vision of an implacably cruel Nature, with man able only to stand and look on helplessly. Now he shows how man can act alongside Nature, as a custodian and as a kind of partner. Farming is all about man collaborating with the natural world, with animals, the soil, landscape and the elements, and it is that collaboration that Hughes emphasizes, perhaps because he had discovered it anew through living in Devon and working alongside Jack Orchard.

Orchard is the subject of several poems, including 'A Monument', 'A Memory', 'Hands' and the very moving 'The Day He Died'. This latter poem is an elegy in the great English tradition. The old man has died just before Valentine's Day, and the land is frost-bound:

> Earth toast-crisp. The snowdrops battered.
> Thrushes spluttering. Pigeons gingerly
> Rubbing their voices together, in stinging cold.
> Crows creaking, and clumsily
> Cracking loose.

> > (CP 533)

All the world is still, unable to move in the cold that is at the same time both physical and emotional. In the last lines, even the land itself is depicted as mourning, coming slowly to terms with the loss, with the realization that it too 'will have to manage without him.' But although the poem ends with the image of a great blankness, there are signs of hope throughout. The day he died, 'was the silkiest day of the young year'; the spring will return, the cattle waiting patiently for their hay will be fed, the moon and the planets will continue to revolve.

Hughes's closeness to the natural world, which runs as a central theme through his writing, is ironically one of the points of division between him and Sylvia Plath. In *Birthday Letters*, 'The Rabbit Catcher' offers a glimpse into one such moment. The poet and his wife have quarrelled, and in a state of 'simmering truce' they go out for a picnic. Walking along the cliff-top, they come across a line of rabbit snares. Without speaking, Plath tears it out of the ground and throws it away. The speaker is appalled:

> I was aghast. Faithful
> To my country gods – I saw
> The sanctity of a trapline desecrated.
> You saw blunt fingers, blood in the cuticles,
> Clamped round a blue mug. I saw
> Country poverty raising a penny,
> Filling a Sunday stewpot. You saw baby-eyed
> Strangled innocents, I saw
> Ancient custom.

> (*BL* 145)

Plath tears up all the snares, in tears of rage, calling the trap-setters murderers. Hughes contrasts her reaction with his own sense of shock, seeing the setting of traps as part of his heritage, a heritage with a long history of peasants struggling to survive off the land. Rabbit-catching was a hard-won concession 'from the hangings and transportation/To live off the land.' Steeped in this history, he cannot hear her or understand her, and she, from a different world, cannot understand him. As with the fox-cub, the poet understands that something irrevocable has happened: 'In those snares/ You'd caught something'. What she has caught is poetry, but it is a writing that can only come out of the abyss that divides them. In this poem, as in 'Your Paris', Hughes exposes the unbridgeable cultural divide be-tween him and Plath, a gap that can only be fully recognized with the clarity provided by hindsight.

*Birthday Letters* restored popular perceptions of Hughes as a passionate and contentious poet, but it should not be forgotten that he produced some very fine work that never received much media attention. A great deal of his work is not particularly well-known, eclipsed by the success of some of the award-winning collections and by the powerful and disturbing Crow poems. Among the lesser-known but very beautiful collections that also show how his writing about the natural environment had changed and matured over time are *River* published in 1983 (revised and extended as *Three Books* in 1993) and *Flowers and Insects* that appeared in 1986. In his notes to *Three Books*, Hughes explains how his fascination for water and for fishing had begun in his childhood:

> It is not easy to separate the fascination of rivers from the fascination of fish. Making dams, waterfalls, water-gardens, water-courses is deeply absorbing play, for most of us, but the results have to be a home for something. When the water is wild, inhabitants are even more important. Streams, rivers, ponds, lakes *without fish* communicate to me one of the ultimate horrors – the poisoning of the wells, death at the source of all that is meant by water.[11]

Hughes's revulsion for the contamination of the environment is more apparent in his later work, though as he indicates in these notes he had understood the detrimental impact of industrial, man-made pollution from early boyhood. The poems in *River* are celebratory- of fish, of water, of the life cycle of all rivers. The different moods that a river can arouse are evoked: in 'Last Night' the river is sinister, a place where 'evil came up/ Out of its stillest holes'. The poet stands in the water, experiencing 'The strange evil/ Of unknown fish-minds'. Yet at other times the mood is completely different. In 'Low Water', the river is a 'beautiful idle woman', who eyes the man standing in the shallows 'steadily from the beginning of the world.' In 'Fairy Flood' the river goddess is a runaway daughter, escaping from the domination of her 'fatherly landscape' and rushing down to the sea. 'September' opens with a statement and goes on to stress the age-old quality of the river goddess, now in her crone aspect:

> There's another river. In this river
> Whose grandmotherly, earth-gnarled, sweetened hands

Welcome me with tremblings, give me the old feel
Of reality's reassurance –
There's a fishy nostalgia.

(CP 674–5)

The poems in *River* show how far Hughes has matured as a poet from the dynamic, yet convoluted language of *The Hawk in the Rain*. He still uses compound nouns, still draws upon his dialect heritage and the rhythms and sonoric patterns of earlier varieties of English, but does so in a manner so much more controlled that it appears effortless. That same quality of writing is evident in *Flowers and Insects*, a collection full of striking images, less lyrical than *River*, perhaps because in writing about fishing Hughes was writing about something very close to himself. The flowers are personified in different, often comical ways. 'Narcissi', for example are represented as children in old-fashioned dress from silent films around Armistice Day in 1918, with pinched faces and wearing floppy ribbon bows. In 'Cyclamens in a Bowl', the flowers are depicted as butterflies 'caught by an uptwisting/Slender snake and held'. The iris in 'Sketch of a Goddess' is a 'Halberd/Of floral complications', while the 'Big Poppy' is a 'Hot-Eyed Mafia Queen'. There is a strong erotic quality in many of the poems, with the flowers represented as seductive women, but there is also a humorous element. The powerful visual aspect of the poems was complemented by illustrations, watercolours by Leonard Baskin. Though never gentle, Nature in these later collections is not violently hostile and through observing the beauty of rivers or flowers the poet achieves some sense of closure. The river, he writes in the title poem of the collection,

Is a god
Knee-deep among reeds, watching men,
Or hung by the heels down the door of a dam

It is a god, and inviolable,
Immortal. And will wash itself of all deaths.

(CP 664)

31

# 2

'Crow looked at the world':
The Poet as Shaman

Apart from the first and last collections, the volume of poetry that has attracted the most critical attention is a work from Hughes's most troubled period, *Crow: From the Life and Songs of the Crow* that was published in 1970. The book is dedicated to Assia and Shura, who had died in 1969. Over the next four years, more than 20,000 copies were sold, interest fuelled by debates about what some readers saw as an excessive violence in Hughes's poetry, a violence apparent in earlier work but now fore-grounded in the Crow poems. One of the first poems in the collection, for example, 'Lineage' uses Biblical language in a shocking sequence that culminates in the begetting of Crow, 'screaming for blood'. The first four lines offer a nightmarish vision of a world of terror and pain:

> In the beginning was Scream
> Who begat Blood
> Who begat Eye
> Who begat Fear

(C 2)

The dark world of *Crow* fascinated and appalled. Martin Dodsworth saw Hughes as a flawed poet, obsessed by cruelty and destructiveness while Roy Fuller felt that Hughes had produced a language of pathological violence.[1] Stephen Coote is even more dismissive: he states that Hughes has developed 'a self-conscious brutalism', particularly in *Crow*.[2] Views such as these, expressed in popular guides to English literature were very damaging, and the idea of Hughes as a poet addicted to gratuitous violence lasted a long time. Hughes himself had little patience with such reactions; he told Ekbert Faas that he believed forms of violence invoked what he called the 'elemental power circuit of the Universe' and could not be avoided. In his view, English writers of the post-war period wanted to feel cosy and not tap into the more dangerous forces in the world. He, however, being slightly younger, 'was all for opening negotiations with whatever happened to be out there.'[3] Whatever was out there for Hughes meant the violence of animals and humans, the traumas of history and the universal patterns of aggression, retribution and regeneration that recur in myths and legends told and retold in communities all over the world.

Always fascinated by birds, Hughes's interest in crows had been evident for several years prior to the publication of the collection, and his Crow character seems to be linked to an encounter in 1957 with the American artist Leonard Baskin, with whom he collaborated on various occasions. Well-known as a Holocaust artist, Baskin's work with its macabre imagery appealed to Hughes. Baskin produced a series of drawings of crow-men, and in 1966 he invited Hughes to write some poems to accompany the sequence. Out of this collaboration came *Crow*, and later Hughes and Baskin were to work together on other occasions including most notably *Cave-Birds* which appeared in 1978.

In the interview with Ekbert Faas, Hughes talked at length about the genesis of the Crow poems. In response to a line of questioning by Faas about the increased use of Biblical and mythological material in his poetry after *Wodwo*, Hughes responded that writing poetry means organizing one's inner world in a particular way, using whatever material seems most appropriate:

> You choose a subject because it serves, because you need it. We go on writing poems because one poem never gets the whole account right. There is always something missed. At the end of the ritual up comes a goblin...While we struggle with a fragmentary Orestes some complete Bacchae moves past too deep down to hear. We get news of it later...too late. In the end, one's poems are ragged dirty undated letters from remote battles and weddings and one thing and another.

The creative process is complex: the poet is compelled to go on writing, without complete understanding of what is happening in his own mind. The image of poems as dirty, undated letters from distant places is a powerful one. The poet may strive to understand what leads him to write, but once the process takes him over, rational explanation fails. In the case of *Crow*, Leonard Baskin provided one source of inspiration; Hughes points out that all kinds of other sources were also involved. From his days as an anthropology student at Cambridge, he had been interested in mythology and folkore and in the interface between the primitive and the civilized. Talking to Faas, he disclaimed much knowledge of Western philosophy, and underlined the importance of works from other cultures, most notably the *Bardo Thodol*, the *Tibetan Book of the Dead* in the genesis of *Crow*. The *Bardo Thodol* in Hughes's view is 'basically a shamanistic flight and return'. When asked to expand on his understanding of shamanism, Hughes connects the shaman, the primitive witch-doctor or medicine-man with the poet. A shaman is summoned by a spirit that appears in dreams, and once he receives the summons he cannot refuse, for the alternative is his own death or the death of someone close to him. He has to learn how to enter the spirit-world, a process that can take years of preparation. The shaman needs to enter the spirit world in order to find an answer to a question or a means of healing someone:

> Now this flight to the spirit world he experiences as a dream...and that dream is the basis of the hero story. It is the same basic outline pretty well all over the world, same events, same figures, same situations. It is the skeleton of thousands of folk-tales and myths. And of many narrative poems. The Odyssey, the Divine Comedy, Faust etc. Most narrative poems recount only those other dreams...the dream of the call. Poets usually refuse the call. How are they to accept it? How can a poet become a medicine man and fly to the source and come back and heal or pronounce oracles? Everything among us is against it.

Yet Hughes identifies with the shaman's flight to the spirit world. The Crow poems, he admits 'were usually something of a shock to write', most of the poems 'appeared as I wrote them', 'mostly they wrote themselves quite rapidly'. Telling the story of Crow in prose and verse was the original intention, indeed Hughes acknowledges that though the story led him to write poetry, the poems stand a little apart and have acquired a life of their own. The story that he intended to tell 'was of course the story of Crow, created by God's nightmare's attempt to improve on man.' It was a story that he never finished, though he published other Crow poems after 1970, and in 1978 he brought out *Cave-Birds*, also illustrated by Baskin. What Hughes seems to have been doing with the Crow poems was writing compulsively over quite a long period a sequence of poems that might have become a much larger, 'epic' work than the collection that eventually appeared in print.

Terry Gifford and Neil Roberts point out the great difference between the published version of *Crow* and Hughes's public readings, where he would tell the story of Crow and locate some of his poems in a wider narrative framework.[4] That story is both a mythological and an autobiographical one. Keith Sagar argues that *Crow*, along with *Cave-Birds* and *Gaudete* can be seen as works deriving from a particular period of Hughes's life, following the deaths of Sylvia Plath and Assia Wevill:

> This total identification with the world of animal suffering is part of the atonement which follows his recognition of his own earlier criminality and his ruthless determination through *Crow*, *Cave-Birds*, and *Gaudete* to acknowledge his guilt unconditionally, to identify himself with the suffering of the victim, and to accept whatever punishment his own imagination finds fit. The victim appears in these poems as a female figure, bride, mother or goddess. But since the goddess is all nature, the victim can equally well be presented as an animal; and such poems are equally grounded in autobiographical experience.[5]

The choice of a crow as his protagonist derives from diverse mythological and folkloric sources. Crows are celebrated in stories in many cultures, from Siberia to North America. Crows and ravens, dark carrion-eating birds that flocked to battlefields to gorge themselves on the bodies of slaughtered soldiers are present in Irish legends, in Viking mythology, in Russian folktales. These dark birds were seen as solitary, cruel and cunning, associated with death, unlike other more sociable birds in the corvine family, such as rooks. The ugliness of crows is heightened by their role as carrion-eaters. Talking to Faas, Hughes explains that this ugliness is also part of universal folk mythology. Often a legendary hero wins through to the prize by choosing something ugly rather than something beautiful – opening the lead casket rather than the gold or silver ones, agreeing to ride an old nag rather than a proud stallion. Choosing the least likely option is often part of the testing of the hero. Hughes declares that he threw out the noblest birds of all, the eagles, and chose a crow instead. In 'Crow and the Birds' the eagle soars, swallows swoop, an owl sails by, herons, blue tits, finches and curlews preen themselves in the sunlight, whereas Crow 'spraddled head-down in the beach-garbage, guzzling a dropped ice-cream'.

The ugliness of the Crow is reinforced by the ugliness of the language used to describe it, words like 'guzzling' and 'spraddled'. Hughes explains that writing the poems was a kind of stylistic experiment, an attempt to find a language that would be suited to this disturbing bird:

> The idea was originally just to write his songs, the songs that a Crow would sing. In other words, songs with no music whatsoever, in a super-simple and super-ugly language which would in a way shed everything except just what he wanted to say without any other consideration and that's the basis of the style of the whole thing. I get near it in a few poems.

The language of the Crow poems is a mixture of the colloquial and the ritual; repetition is a much-used device, which gives many of the poems an incantatory effect. 'Examination at the Womb-door', for example is constructed as a series of questions, all answered by the one word, 'Death' until the last two lines, when the question asked is 'But who is stronger than death?' and the answer comes simply 'Me, evidently'. The poem ends with two words: 'Pass, Crow'. The bird is more powerful than death, the riddle has been answered.

*Crow* shows Hughes drawing upon all kinds of poetic forms. 'Snake Hymn' is written in the manner of a medieval carol, 'Song for a Phallus' uses the ballad format, with a refrain after each verse, 'A Bedtime Story' begins with 'Once upon a time...', 'Crow Improvises' uses a familiar nursery-rhyme and nursery-tale form, exemplified in 'The House that Jack Built', where events follow one another in a sequence marked by repeated phrases. The question and answer riddle format is also the framework for 'The Black Beast', where the repeated question is simply ' where is the Black Beast?'. In this poem, Crow's frantic search drives him to a frenzy of destructiveness: he broods, then shouts, then beats on the walls, splits the skull of his enemy, 'crucified a frog under a microscope', 'killed his brother and turned him inside out to stare at his colour', he burns the earth, charges into space driving away the stars, but the question remains unanswered and the final line of the poem repeats it still. The one place where Crow has not looked is inside himself.

Crow's lack of self-knowledge and violent destructive urges recur in poem after poem, yet there is often a glimmer of empathy with the dark, brutish bird and this comes across through the language and the verse forms employed. In 'Glimpse', Crow struggles to express something that may possibly have been a beautiful thought. Inadequate with words, Crow falls back on an archaic, clichéd poetic language that is cut off almost as soon he starts to speak it:

'O leaves', sang Crow, trembling, 'O leaves –'

The touch of a leaf's edge at his throat
Guillotined further comment.

(CP 84)

Whatever glimpse Crow may have had is blocked by the leaf itself, a leaf that slices like a guillotine. Lyricism has no place in Crow's universe of blackness.

In his note on *Crow* that appeared in *Selected Poems 1957–1981*, Hughes writes simply that 'this is a sequence of poems relating the birth, upbringing and adventures of a protagonist of that name'. In a radio interview given in 1970, Hughes expanded that statement pointing out that the main story

takes Crow through a series of experiences which alter him in one way and another, take him to the bottom and then take him to the top, and eventually the whole purpose of the thing is to try to turn him into a man, which, as it stands, the story nearly succeeds in doing, but I haven't completed it, and whether one could complete it I don't know.[6]

Keith Sagar provides an appendix to his book on Ted Hughes, *The Laughter of Foxes* in which he reconstructs the story of Crow, using Hughes's own words, taken from radio broadcasts, essays, letters, readings and, of course, the poems. What this summary shows is that having come into being, as Crow grows, so he struggles for understanding, questioning God, striving to comprehend death and love, wrestling with the power of words. The violence, terror and pain in the world are offset by other more hopeful forces. At some stage in his journey, he meets the ghost of an Eskimo hunter who becomes his spiritual guide. The last poems in *Crow* are 'Two Eskimo Songs' and 'Littleblood', songs taught by the Eskimo guide who believes that good spirits can be passed on through song. These final poems change the mood of *Crow*, and the conclusion is much less dark, much quieter. The wounded creature, Littleblood, that has grown wise 'sucking death's mouldy tits' is invited to share the wisdom: 'Sit on my finger, sing in my ear, O littleblood' in a line resonant with tenderness, if not necessarily with hope.

In their writing about *Crow*, the figure of the trickster, the devilish clown-character that recurs in mythologies around the world is often mentioned by critics. Loki, the Norse God is one example of the trickster character, a figure that appears in North American myth in animal form, as a black bird such as a raven or as a rabbit. The trickster is a kind of clown, a diabolical figure, who presumes to challenge the gods and creates mischief wherever he appears. He has no moral code, he continually tricks gods, men and animals, but at the same time is often tricked himself, for though cunning and wily, he is not necessarily intelligent. The trickster has strong appetites and a childish desire for instant gratification. Trickster stories revolve around jokes played at someone else's expense, or situations in which the trickster comes off worst. What also happens in trickster mythology is that through the cruel jokes, new levels of understanding can sometimes be reached. Often a trickster's action has extraordinary consequences: when Loki casually throws a stone and kills an otter, while walking with Odin and Hoenir, the act unleashes a series of events that will lead to the saga of the ring of Andvari, the basic plot of the *Nibelungenlied*. It is possible that Hughes had this particular story in mind when writing the poems that are placed at the start of the volume, the poems that see the arrival of Crow, for there is a reference to an otter in a stream, followed by a reference to the blackness of gall, the bitterness that follows murder and leads to a cycle of revenge and devastation. 'Two Legends' comprises two poems in which the adjective 'black' is repeated throughout. The first poem is a litany of blackness – 'Black was the without eye', 'black the liver, black the lungs', 'black the blood', 'black too the muscles', 'black also the soul'. In the second poem, the adjective is used for other things than the embryonic Crow. The first three lines take up the image of an otter in a stream, then the poem moves abruptly to an image of death:

> Black is the wet otter's head, lifted.
> Black is the rock, plunging in foam.
> Black is the gall lying on the bed of blood

(C 1)

The forces of the universe, sun and moon hatch Crow, but in this Creation myth order is not made out of chaos, rather emptiness is bent in a black rainbow over emptiness. Nevertheless, what has come into being is alive, as the last two words indicate: 'But flying'. Whatever has been created is in motion. 'The Door' makes that movement more explicit, as Crow comes flying into the world through the black pupil of an eye – 'Flying from sun to sun, he found this home.'

Crow's trickster characteristics are highlighted in several poems. 'A Childish Prank' is built around an archetypal trickster story. God has created man and woman, bodies without souls and ponders on the next step. Now Crow intervenes:

> Crow laughed.
> He bit the Worm, God's only son,
> Into two writhing halves.

(C 8)

Crow takes these two halves, stuffs the tail end into the man 'With the wounded end hanging out', then stuffs the other end of the Worm into the woman, where it crawls up inside her 'to peer out through her eyes.' The half within woman calls out to its other half:

> Man awoke being dragged across the grass.
> Woman awoke to see him coming.
> Neither knew what had happened.

(C 8)

Crow has invented sexual desire, has condemned God's creatures to suffering, for the two divided halves try to reunite 'because O it was painful'. The poem ends with God still asleep, Crow still laughing at what he has done. As with many of the

39

Crow poems, the brutal imagery is offset by a kind of black humour. The story of Crow biting the serpent in half and, in good Yorkshire English, stuffing the two parts into man and woman is bleakly comic. The last line of the poem reinforces that comedy. Time and again Hughes uses a strong final line in the same way as Shakespeare used a final couplet in his sonnets, to give an ironic twist to what has gone before. A particularly good example of this technique can be found in 'A Horrible Religious Error,' another poem about man, woman and the serpent. The 'earth-bowel brown' serpent emerges, God grimaces, man and woman fall on their knees, but Crow is unmoved:

> Then took a step or two forward,
> Grabbed this creature by the slackskin nape,
>
> Beat the hell out of it and ate it.

(C 37)

This final line, in colloquial English that contrasts with the archaic compound adjective 'slackskin' in the previous line is grotesquely comic. Crow reacts instinctively, once again destroying whatever God may have planned. Crow's complete lack of any kind of moral understanding is a recurrent theme. In 'Crow's First Lesson', God tries to teach Crow language, but fails miserably. The word God tries to make Crow understand is 'Love'. God's first attempt leads to the creation of the white shark out of Crow's gaping mouth, the second attempt creates plague-bearing insects. God tries for a third and last time, and out of Crow's convulsed retchings comes 'Man's prodigious head'. Then Crow completes the grim process of creation:

> And Crow retched again, before God could stop him.
> And woman's vulva dropped over man's neck and
> > Tightened.
> The two struggled together on the grass.

(C 9)

God struggles to separate man and woman, cursing and weeping, while the last line states simply that 'Crow flew guiltily off.' God's endeavours to teach Crow his first word have resulted in the creation of destructive forces, savage animals, deadly diseases and the vicious conflict between man and woman that God is powerless to resolve.

Hughes gives us the figure of God as an incompetent, inadequate creator and depicts human sexuality as a cruel war-game. In 'Crow Communes', God is described as 'a great carcase'. In 'Crow Blacker than Ever', God retreats, 'disgusted with man,' while man also retreats, 'disgusted with God' and turns instead to woman. Crow's reaction is to nail man and God together, so that each cries out with the other's voice, bleeds with the other's blood, because 'man could not be man nor God God' and the universe 'became gangrenous and stank'. In this 'horror beyond redemption', Crow grins and proclaims it all his creation. Again, the last line highlights the poem's ironic message, for as Crow makes his declaration he is 'flying the black flag of himself'. God and man are joined in suffering, but Crow can be himself and fly on. In a recording made in 1973, Hughes explains more about God:

> This particular God, of course, is the man-created, broken down, corrupt despot of a ramshackle religion, who bears about the same relationship to the Creator as, say, ordinary English does to reality.[7]

By the end of *Crow* God has faded away and the emphasis has shifted to the agony of man and woman, locked in their sadistic sexual conflict. 'Notes for a Little Play' is constructed around the image of two survivors of a final nuclear holocaust, who sniff one another out:

> They fasten together. They seem to be eating each other.
> But they are not eating each other.
> They do not know what else to do.

(C 80)

The creatures 'dance a strange dance', they celebrate a marriage 'in the darkness of the sun', but it is a celebration, as the final line warns, 'without guest or God'. The following poem, 'Snake Hymn' depicts a world without God, a world in which the Christian myths have come undone, and sexual desire in all its brutality is the only force in the universe. 'Lovesong', which comes straight after 'Snake Hymn' makes this even more explicit. Here love is a hideous destructive process. The lovers bite and gnaw one another, suck each other dry, nail one another down. Their encounters are depicted through a string of images of violence:

41

His words were occupying armies
Her laughs were assassin's attempts
His looks were bullets daggers of revenge
Her glances were ghosts in the corner with horrible secrets
His whispers were whips and jackboots

(C 82)

The lovers dismember one another, take one another over, become each other in a process of savage metamorphosis. God is helpless, love is nothing but violent sexual aggression, human beings are caught up in a cycle of desire that leads to their own destruction. Faced with such knowledge, the irony of Crow struggling to find words in 'Glimpse' is even more bitter.

It is important to remember the historical context within which Hughes was working in the 1960s and early 1970s. He has drawn attention himself to the particular mood of the post-war period, with the anxiety generated by fears of a nuclear holocaust and memories of the previous two wars still very present in people's minds. Though few poets seemed prepared to tackle overtly political themes, the situation in the theatre was completely different. One of the most exciting developments in London in the 1960s was the World Theatre Season, and translations of plays by writers such as Eugene Ionesco and Samuel Beckett brought surrealist and absurdist ideas to the attention of English audiences. The playwrights of the so-called Theatre of the Absurd wrote about a world that no longer made sense, a world where belief and security did not exist. In 1964, inspired by Antonin Artaud, Peter Brook, with whom Hughes was to collaborate, directed Peter Weiss's play, *The Persecution and Assassination of Jean-Paul Marat as Performed by the Inmates of the Asylum of Charenton under the Direction of Monsieur de Sade*. The *Marat-Sade,* as the play became known, heralded Brook's Theatre of Cruelty season. He had directed *King Lear* in 1962, a play that explores the depths of human suffering, and in 1966 he directed *US*. Hughes translated Seneca's *Oedipus* for Brook which was produced in 1968. These productions share a great deal with *Crow* in that black comedy is combined with profound questioning, and the comedy offsets the savagery of the actions and events that are represented. Laughter is not pitiless in such a context, but it highlights the tragic absurdity of the human predicament.

'Crow Tyrannosaurus' is a good example of Hughes's use of black comedy. The images of death in the poem are particularly repulsive: the body of a dead bird pulsates with maggots, a cat's body writhes in agony, a dog is 'a bulging filterbag/ Of all the deaths it had gulped for the flesh and the bones'. Man is 'a walking /Abattoir,' and Crow understands that all these creatures have killed in order to eat. Faced with this horror, Crow wonders whether he ought to find another way: 'To stop eating?And try to become the light.' No sooner does he pose this question, than he sees a source of food:

> But his eye saw a grub. And his head, trapsprung, stabbed.
> And he listened
> And he heard
> Weeping
>
> Grubs grubs   He stabbed   he stabbed
> Weeping
> Weeping
>
> Weeping he walked and stabbed

(C 14)

Crow follows his instinct, which is to kill and eat and survive. He can do nothing else, and the grim laughter comes in the contrast between his realization that this is what he must do and the act of killing. As he stabs his prey, he weeps, and Crow's weeping is reminiscent of Lewis Carroll's Walrus, weeping into a pocket handkerchief as he swallows the oysters he has invited to walk with him. Crow is still a stranger to pity.

Laughter seems to take on a life of its own in some of the Crow poems. 'A Grin' is an absurdist poem about a disembodied grin, trying to find a permanent home. It tries out different faces – the face of a woman in childbirth, a man caught in a car crash, a machine-gunner about to die, a steeplejack falling to his death, two lovers at the moment of orgasm, but none of these last. Then the grin tries 'the face /Of somebody lost in sobbing', a murderer's face and the face of man destroying everything around him. Finally it tries the face of a man about to die in the electric chair, 'but that too relaxed'. The poem ends with the grin at a loss, stripped back to its essence, to its existence on a skull:

The grin
Sank back, temporarily nonplussed,
Into the skull.

(C 19)

A variation on the same theme is found in 'In Laughter'. Here too is a litany of horrors, car crashes, sinking ships, dismemberment, a meteorite crashing down onto a baby's pram, and through all this laughter 'scampers round on centipede boots' until it becomes exhausted, 'Like somebody the police have come for'. Similarly, 'The Smile' travels around the world, through time, 'Looking for its occasion' and finds it, just for a second, in the face of a suffering man at the point of death.

The arrangement of the poems in *Crow* has its own logic, despite the existence of many other Crow poems and Hughes's remarks about the relationship between these poems and the story of Crow more generally. After the genesis of Crow, the quest begins for some kind of understanding of creation. This is the shamanic journey, and a series of poems focusing on language connects Crow's quest to that of a poet. In 'Crow's First Lesson', God fails to teach Crow language; later, in 'Crow Communes', Crow asks questions of a snoring, unconscious God. When God does not answer, Crow tears off a mouthful and asks pompously:

'Will this cipher divulge itself to digestion
Under hearing beyond understanding?'

(C 20)

He asks this as a joke, but 'suddenly felt much stronger'. This new-found strength, though, leads him nowhere. He sits 'Half-illumined. Speechless' and in the final line 'appalled'.

Crow is still appalled, still reflecting in 'A Disaster'. Crow hears 'news of a word', but sees that word killing men, destroying cities, polluting the world. The word is compared to a giant lamprey, sucking the earth dry. Words attack Crow in the next poem, 'The Battle of Osfrontalis', but by 'Crow Goes Hunting' he has learned enough to try and use words to his own advantage. He imagines words as a pack of hounds, chasing a hare, and in classic folk-tale mode, the hare changes itself into a series of different objects, forcing Crow to change words into other objects that can pursue it. So the hare becomes a concrete bunker, Crow turns words into bombs, the bunker becomes a flock of starlings, the words become shotguns, the starlings transform into a cloudburst, words become a reservoir to collect the water, the reservoir turns into an earthquake and swallows the reservoir before it turns back into a hare and escapes, 'having eaten Crow's words. Watching the hare run, Crow is 'speechless with admiration'. The natural world is more powerful than the word, the mystery of the hare is indefinable.

Early reactions to *Crow* as a poetry of violence and nihilism missed the point of Hughes's work. The violence is certainly present, but it is never gratuitous and there is a strong comic strain of black humour that mitigates against the more extreme images of horror. *Crow* is important, not because it signals a change in Hughes's writing, though clearly the poems do mark a shift from his earlier work, but because it is so obviously a synthesis of ideas, images, and stories from an eclectic variety of sources. Those who see *Crow* as reflecting a darker phase in Hughes's life following the deaths of the two women he loved are right to some extent, but what *Crow* shows is a writer wrestling with profound existential questions and experimenting with new forms. By the end of the volume Crow is a monarch reigning over a vast empty kingdom of silence. God, mankind, words have all failed to give Crow the answer, but 'Glimpse', the poem placed just before the last poem in which Crow features, 'King of Carrion', shows Crow struggling to make poetry, failing, but nevertheless continuing to stare at the leaves, 'Through the god's head instantly substituted'. The two Eskimo songs along with 'Littleblood' provide a kind of epilogue. In 'Fleeing from Eternity' man gives woman eyes and a mouth with which to weep blood and cry pain, that is to live, in exchange for song, and feels 'the song was worth it'. Woman feels cheated, but the song has come into being. The second song, 'How Water Began to Play' tells the story of water that wanted to live and goes through the world, to the sun, to flowers, three times to the womb, to stone and through all space, each time 'it came weeping back' until

> It lay at the bottom of all things
> Utterly worn out                    utterly clear.

(C 88)

45

Through suffering comes clarity; this is the answer that the questor sought. The concluding poem, 'Littleblood' echoes the famous Latin poem addressing his soul by the Emperor Hadrian. 'O littleblood, little boneless little skinless' recalls 'animula vagula blandula' 'little soul wandering gentle soul'. The tiny creature that is undefined has become wise through suffering, and is invited to sing in the ear of the poet in the concluding image of the volume: 'Sit on my finger, sing in my ear, O Littleblood'. The writer will always find a way to write again, no matter how painful the process and how long the search for a voice.

The mythological sources of *Crow* are manifold, but there are also important literary ones. He and Daniel Weissbort had founded *Modern Poetry in Translation* in 1967 and as can be seen from the many reviews he wrote in the 1960s he was reading work by writers from many different cultural backgrounds. Among the writers he discovered whose work he admired was Vasko Popa, and he wrote an introduction to the Penguin edition of Popa's *Selected Poems*. What appealed to Hughes in Popa's writing and in the work of other Eastern European writers was the ability to go beyond suffering, to aspire to life even in the most extreme circumstances. Such writers, Hughes felt, had 'managed to accept a view of 'the unaccommodated Universe' without becoming cynical, they had gone back to the 'simple animal courage of accepting the odds and have rediscovered the frontier'.[8] Of Popa, Hughes writes admiringly about his ability to combine different elements in his writing, being on the one hand a 'sophisticated philosopher,' on the other 'a primitive gnomic spellmaker':

> The whole style is a marvellously effective artistic invention. It enables Popa to be as abstract as man can be, yet remain as intelligible and as entertaining and as fully human as if he were telling a comic story. It is in this favourite device of his, the little fable or visionary surrealism to the far older and deeper thing, the surrealism of folklore.

He goes on to explain this distinction: literary surrealism, in his view, is concerned with moving away from the practicalities of living, whereas folktale surrealism is always 'urgently connected with the business of trying to manage practical difficulties', hence it has a down-to-earth quality that Hughes admires. It is possible to see Hughes emulating this kind of writing in *Crow*, drawing inspiration from Popa and from other writers who had found a coherent way of surviving extremes and writing without cynicism.

Mythology, world folklore, Eastern European poetry, Shakespeare's *King Lear*, children's verse, the absurd world of writers such as Beckett, Weiss and Ionesco all served to differing degrees as sources of inspiration to Hughes. His shamanic quest can be seen to be also a quest that took him on a journey through the work of writers and story-tellers from cultures distant in both space and time. What also starts to become apparent from this period onwards is Hughes's fascination for the ancient world, for the Latin and Greek foundation texts that had provided part of the bedrock upon which English literature had been built. Greek mythology is very evident in *Crow*, the Oedipus myth in particular. 'Crowego' has Crow following Ulysses and then devouring him, acquiring an electrode in his brain made from Hercules' ashes, drinking Beowulf's blood, communing 'with poltergeists out of old ponds'. Crow gazes into 'the quag of the past' in order to see the future, and the poem ends with the image of a leopard, a creature of great symbolic significance to Hughes, prowling in a fat land. Leopards and jaguars are symbols of elemental energy, violent and beautiful beasts that, like William Blake's Tiger have what he calls a 'summoning force'. 'Crowego' is therefore a poem about the power of literature: Crow has devoured the ancients, both Greek and Anglo-Saxon and now gazes into the future like a leopard. It is not too far-fetched to read this poem as a statement about writing. Hughes, like Crow, has eaten and is ready to move on, 'himself the only page'.

47

# 3

'Being British is the mystery':
Hughes and his English Roots

In 1979 Hughes published *Remains of Elmet*, subtitled 'A Pennine Sequence' in an edition illustrated with photographs by Fay Godwin. The book is dedicated to his mother Edith and in his prefatory note, Hughes explains the impulses that lay behind its creation. He generously attributes his inspiration to Fay Godwin, suggesting that her photographs of the Yorkshire landscape moved him to write poems to accompany them, though he had in fact always been inspired by the landscapes of his childhood as can be seen even in his first collection of poems. He made three subsequent versions of the sequence of poems, the last simply entitled *Elmet* in 1994.

In the preface, he also traces the history of that particular Yorkshire valley, a history that goes back into ancient times. As with his philosophy of language, that connects his own Yorkshire speech with Middle English, so Hughes draws links between the contemporary and the past, stressing the individualism of the local people. The Calder Valley 'was the last ditch of Elmet, the last British Celtic kingdom to fall to the Angles'.[1] The inhabitants of the valley are therefore the descendants of a warrior race, a Celtic tribe who resisted invaders to the end. That fierce heritage lived on: Hughes relates how for centuries the valley was a lawless place, until the Industrial Revolution in the eighteenth century transformed it into a hub of textile production. In the post-industrial age that Hughes inhabits, all those histories are unravelling:

> Throughout my lifetime, since 1930, I have watched the mills of the region and their attendant chapels die. Within the last fifteen years

the end has come. They are now virtually dead, and the population of the valley and the hillsides, so rooted for so long, is changing rapidly.[2]

The starting point then is loss: the death of a way of life, the end of a long period of proud resistance, the dispersal of a population that carries traces of its ancient heritage within. Yet critics such as Ann Skea and Keith Sagar have drawn attention to the prevalence of images of light in this collection, Sagar going so far as to suggest that these poems show the distance that Hughes has 'travelled from the world of blood to the world of light'.[3] Violence has been replaced with elegy, with a lament for a vanishing world.

A sense of mourning pervades this collection. In 'Walls at Alcomden', stone walls built by 'exhilarated men' have crumbled – 'here is the hulk, every rib shattered', and only 'a few crazed sheep' are left. Farms are dead in 'Shackleton Hill', the land is 'naked now as a wound' in 'Wadsworth Moor'. Farms are like 'melting corpses' in' The Sheep Went on being Dead', and hikers have replaced the mill-workers and farmers who kept the valley alive. In 'Remains of Elmet' that same message is reinforced by a string of images that personify the man-made constructions in landscape, representing them as grotesquely voracious creatures. The farms are 'stony masticators', eating each other, while 'the sunk mill-towns' devour everything that comes into contact with them. Through the remains of the ruined world come 'tourists, to pick among crumbling, loose molars/ And empty sockets'. This final image returns us to the opening image where Hughes envisions the Calder Valley as a great gullet, created aeons ago in the 'death-struggle of the glacier'. Formed violently in the Ice Age, the valley has continued to devour all with which it comes into contact.

Along with these elegiac poems about the physical fabric of the Calder Valley are more explicitly autobiographical poems, scenes from Hughes's childhood – a cricket match, a game of football, a boy fishing in a polluted canal, walking to school past the factory, exploring the frightening darkness of a damp tunnel. Along with the images of childhood are the ever-present old men, survivors of wars and a lifetime of hard labour in the mills, who watch the world changing with stoicism and resignation. In 'Crown Point Pensioners' the old men with their

49

flat caps and walking sticks are 'attuned to each other, like the strings of a harp', they are story-tellers from a lost age, 'singers of a lost kingdom'. Above them planes fly, symbols of modernity, bound for America, below them 'moor-water toils in the valley' as it has done for ever. In 'Heptonstall' the village is personified as one of these old men, suffering from amnesia, losing interest in the world around him, sitting alone listening to the ticking of a clock, 'heart good for nothing now', waiting to die.

One of the most powerful poems in the collection is explicitly autobiographical. 'The Dark River' is about both the living and the dead: in the opening lines of the poem, an old man's response to an invitation to a cup of tea summons up the poet's dead mother: 'Six years into her posthumous life/ My uncle raises my mother's face'. Summoning up his dead mother is the starting point for the volume. In that simple ritual exchange, Hughes is briefly united through his uncle with his own past, a past that is personified in the figure of his mother but which also is intimately linked to the place where he and the old man were born:

> And the smoky valley never closes,
> The womb that bore him, chimney behind chimney,
> Horizons herded – behind encircling horizons,
> A happy hell, the arguing, immortal dead,
> The hymns rising past farms.

> (CP 455)

The poet's 'last inheritance' are the memories stirred by the old uncle's stories, 'archaeology of the mouth', as he shares his memories from the last eighty years. Those memories are connected to Hughes, and the phrase 'attached to me' is used deliberately twice to emphasize the bond between the two of them:

> Keeping their last eighty years alive and attached to me.
> Keeping their strange depths alive and attached to me.

> (CP 455)

The imagery of dark water that recurs so often in Hughes's poetry, connected here as elsewhere to memories of fishing is the one that concludes the poem. The old man remembers a huge fish, and now the poet does also, though 'on such a frayed, fraying hair-fineness' that at any moment it could vanish forever, folded back into the dark river. That river is both an actual river and the mythical river Lethe, the river of forgetfulness. What binds Hughes to the old region of Elmet are the people and the memories they stir in him, but just as the stone buildings are crumbling back into the earth, so the generation he remembers and whose memories have in turn shaped him are all dying. In 'Hepstonstall Old Church' he allegorizes this message in the last four lines:

> The crystal in men's heads
> Blackened and fell to pieces.
>
> The valleys went out.
> The moorland broke loose.

(CP 490)

Thomas West is one of the few critics who singles out *Remains of Elmet* for special praise. He suggests that the collection brings together life, history and real places 'mythically with the writer, whose poetry is at times close to an exalted form of remembering'.[4] He argues that in this collection Hughes combines personal memory with folk memory, in what can be considered 'his tribe's memorial', a view that is supported by Hughes's own preface, in which he explains that gradually he came to realize that he was, in fact, living among the survivors in the ruins of what remained. The poet's task is then to record his own memories, along with the memories of the survivors and at the same time to record aspects of the story of the place, a story that stretches back into prehistoric times.

This combination of micro and macro histories is an important element in Hughes's writing. Running through his work, from *The Hawk in the Rain* onwards is a strong sense of English history and an even stronger awareness of his own roots. *Remains of Elmet* is a collection of poems about a place, and it is also a meditation on the poet's family, in particular his mother. For if Hughes had been profoundly influenced by the men in his family and their stories about the First World War, so his mother, with her Celtic heritage, her claims to psychic powers and her story-telling skills had played a major role in his formative years. Significantly, he chose to dedicate the book to Edith Farrar, using his mother's maiden name. Farrar is also the second name given to his son Nicholas. That name had a particular resonance:

51

among Edith Farrar's ancestors could have been Robert Farrar, an Anglican bishop burned at the stake in 1555 for his beliefs during the Marian persecutions and Nicholas Ferrar [sic] who in the seventeenth century founded a religious community at Little Gidding, which T.S. Eliot was later to write about so movingly in *Four Quartets*.

'The Martyrdom of Bishop Farrar' is included in *The Hawk in the Rain*. It stands out from the other poems, both in terms of the content and in terms of the richly convoluted language, but once the connection is made to Hughes's own history, then its appropriateness in this first collection becomes apparent. Robert Farrar refused to compromise, refused to stop preaching what was regarded by the authorities as heresy and went to his death insisting on the rightness of his beliefs. Before going to the stake, he declared that if he should cry out during the burning, the doctrine he had preached should not be believed, and the bishop's last words are given as a preface to Hughes's poem. His life and his death testify to the power of the word:

> Words which, before they will be dumbly spared,
> Will burn their body and be tongues with fire
> Make paltry folly of flesh and this world's air.

> (HR 62)

Just as the ancestor was prepared to die rather than recant, so the young poet makes his own heretical poetic statement.

Hughes celebrates Nicholas Ferrer in a poem of that name in *Lupercal*. Here, though, the mood and the language are very different, and prefigure *Remains of Elmet*. Nicholas Ferrer has withdrawn from the world: not for him the public proclamation and the bold rebellion, rather the quietness of a rural community dedicated to God, where pigs and hay and well-thumbed bibles are the reality.

Religion in different guises appears repeatedly in Hughes's work, often through its symbolic constructions – churches, chapels, memorials and cemeteries. Hughes is interested in the architecture of religion, in the way in which a landscape could be altered by the arrival of new ideas. The preface to *Remains of Elmet* records the impact of Methodism on the valley, especially the preaching of Parson Grimshaw, the late-eighteenth century preacher of Haworth. Hughes is in no doubt about the effect

Grimshaw's brand of religion had on the community:

> To judge by the shock-wave, which could still be felt, I think, well
> into this century, he struck the whole region 'like a planet'...To a
> degree, he changed the very landscape. His heavenly fire, straight
> out of Blakes's *Prophetic Books*, shattered the terrain into biblical
> landmarks: quarries burst open like craters, and chapels the bedrock
> transfigured – materialized standing in them.[5]

In 'Mount Zion' the inheritors of Grimshaw's brand of religious
zealotry are described as 'a mesmerized commissariat', the
women 'bleak as Sunday rose-gardens', the men 'in their prison-
yard, at attention, /Exercising their cowed, shaven souls'. This
religion is terrifying, the dark mass of the chapel blocks the
moon and outside the kitchen window it is a 'gravestone slab', 'a
deadfall'.

With the advent of Methodism, the dark stone of the valley
would be used to construct chapels and the men who built them
also built the mills that would bring a new world of industry
with them. Hughes notes how the builders placed their
'massive, stone, prison-like structures' on the edge of cliffs. In
'Under the World's Wild Rims' Hughes remembers walking to
school in the shadow of the mills – 'five hundred glass skylights,
a double row/ Watched me, across the canal'. Now, though, the
age of the mills is ended. In 'Mill Ruins' the 'great humming
abbeys' that were once workplaces are described as tombs. In
'First, Mills' the coming of industry and the railways is seen as a
fatal wound to the valley:

> First, Mills
> And steep wet cobbles
> Then cenotaphs.
>
> First, football pitches, crown greens
> Then the bottomless wound of the railway station
> That bled this valley to death.
>
> The fatal wound.
>
> (CP 462)

The railway that served as the means of transporting manu-
factured products out of the valley, serves also to transport its
youth away to war, as the outside world makes its demands
heard. And the coming of the mills means also a new way of life,

one that confines men and women in stone prisons. 'Hill-stone was content' is an ironic poem, in which the stones themselves are seen as colluding with the incarceration of human beings:

> It let itself be conscripted
> Into mills. And it stayed in position
> Defending this slavery against all.

(CP 463)

The stones forget their roots in the earth, while the men who work in the mills become 'fixed, like the stones', resigned to their fate. The word 'conscripted' is a reminder of the ever-present thread in Hughes' poetry of the devastating impact of the First World War on small communities. Dennis Walder, in his introductory guide to Hughes's poetry suggests that he could equally be labelled as a nature poet or a war poet. However, unlike poets writing directly out of their own wartime experience

> He is a war poet at one remove, writing out of the impact of memory – the individual memory of his father, and the collective memory of English culture.[6]

There is a sequence of war poems in *The Hawk in the Rain*, 'Six Young Men' is inspired by a photograph, now 'faded and ochre-tinged'. The first stanza sketches what can be seen in the photograph, the different poses that suggest different character-types. The second stanza moves into the present. The men are all 'trimmed for a Sunday jaunt', and the poet tells us that he knows exactly where they had gone. The bank, the trees, the black wall are unchanged in forty years, and the sound the water makes as it pours downhill is likewise unchanged. Then the tone of the poem darkens: the next two stanzas detail how some of them died, 'the rest, nobody knows what they came to, . . ./all were killed'. The poem moves onto another stage in the final stanza, when the language with its Shakespearean echoes changes and the reader is addressed directly:

> That man's not more alive whom you confront
> And shake by the hand, see hale, hear speak out loud,
> Than any of these six celluloid smiles are

(HR 57)

54

The men in the photograph live on; yet the next line tells us the opposite: they are more dead than prehistoric creatures. The photograph offers 'contradictory permanent horrors'. The poet cannot avoid knowing that the smiling men died horribly decades ago, nor can he escape the fact that the place where they enjoyed their Sunday outing is also his place, still recognizably the same. The past is embedded in the present, inescapably.

In *Wodwo* Hughes writes specifically about his father, one of the survivors of the Gallipoli campaign. 'Out' is a poem in three parts, which combines realistic detail with surrealist elements and ranges across time, moving from a memory of the poet as a four-year-old watching his father brooding over buried memories of war to time present, as Hughes refuses to buy a Remembrance Day poppy. The first part of the poem is subtitled 'The Dream Time'; Hughes's father is pictured sitting in his chair by the fireside, silently 'recovering/ From the four-year mastication by gunfire and mud'. Since he will not speak openly of his experiences and the child is in any case too young to understand, what happens is a process of fantasizing memory. The child who becomes the adult poet gleans certain things about his father's experiences and then grafts those memories onto what he later learns:

> While I, small and four,
> Lay on the carpet as his luckless double,
> His memories buried, immovable anchor,
> Among jawbones and blown-off boots, tree-stumps,
>           shellcases and craters,
> Under rain that goes on drumming its rods and thickening
> Its kingdom, which the sun has abandoned, and where
>                     nobody
> Can ever move from shelter.

> (*CP* 165)

The child is compelled to take into himself images of a war that happened long before he was born, but which lives on in his father's mind. The grim images of body parts, mud and rain and a world without hope are handed on to the 'luckless' son as his legacy. This is a history from which there can be no escape.

The second section of the poem shifts from images of the

battlefield to a dead body in a cave, juxtaposed with a woman giving birth. Birth and death are inextricably bound up with one another, and the dead man, now specifically an 'infantryman' is 'reassembled' in some kind of monstrous process of regeneration that reminds us of the cycle of monstrosity whereby infants are born only to grow up and be sent off to die on distant killing-fields. The nurse wraps up the new-born, the mother smiles faintly but the poem reminds us that 'it's just another baby'. The last four lines reinforce that message: the baby may grow up to be an ordinary man until extraordinary events precipitate him into horror:

> As after being blasted to bits
> The reassembled infantryman
> Tentatively totters out, gazing round with the eyes
> Of an exhausted clerk.

> (CP 166)

In the final section, 'Remembrance Day', Hughes develops a subject that recurs elsewhere in his writing – the memorializing of the dead, through monuments and ceremonies, which he sees as fundamentally dishonest. The poppies sold on Remembrance Day are described as whores. The poet returns to the story of his own father, hit by shrapnel that miraculously did not kill him because it struck his pocket-book and deflected the impact. The story of that survival has been told so many times that the poet claims he is gripped by it, just as in his youth he felt weighted down by more of his father's stories. At the close of the poem he is trying to free himself from the dead weight of his father's past that is also England's legacy

> You dead bury your dead.
> Goodbye to the cenotaphs on my mother's breasts.
> Goodbye to all the remaindered charms of my father's survival.
>
> Let England close. Let the green sea-anemone close.

> (CP 166)

Years later, in 1993, Hughes published another poem about his father and the First World War. 'The Last of the 1st/15th Lancashire Fusiliers' is subtitled 'A Souvenir of the Gallipoli Landings'. The mood of the poem is very different from that of 'Out', there is much less anger though still a strong sense of personal engagement. A man's sons watch him as he crosses a courtyard, his limping gait making him seem like a bird, 'a water-bird, an ibis going over pebbles', 'a long-billed, spider-kneed bird/Bow-backed, finding his footing'. They laugh, but now they cannot remember why they laughed, and the memory of their laughter makes them want to weep:

> As after the huge wars
>
> Senseless huge wars
>
> Huge senseless weeping.

(CP 850–1)

Whereas in 'Out' the enforced memory of war that the poet cannot escape from, that has been programmed into him since early childhood is presented as painfully immediate, a bleeding wound that keeps reopening, here the pain is of a different kind. The poet laments the senselessness of war, rather than struggling with his own personal anguish. The agony has turned into grief, and what is remembered here is not a child's litany of imagined battlefield horrors, but the unthinking laughter of boys watching a damaged man with a limp through a window. Their laughter is compared to warships with fluttering bunting, decorated warships 'where war is only an idea, as drowning is only an idea'. The camaraderie of men at war is depicted as 'a kind of careless health', and his father is a man who 'once held war in his strong pint mugful of tea/And drank at it, heavily sugared'. Now, with that careless health long since destroyed, he 'has become a bird', has metamorphosed into an ungainly creature whose sons find him amusing. The senseless and pity of war are brought together in the image of the awkward bird and the unfeeling laughter.

Memories of war are present also in *Wolfwatching*, (1989). 'Dust As We Are' begins with the familiar image of the silent father and the watching child:

> My post-war father was so silent
> He seemed to be listening. I eavesdropped
> On the hot line. His lonely sittings
> Mangled me, in secret – like T.V.

(CP 753)

This admission of the damage done to the young Hughes is

developed in the second stanza, where the poet admits 'I had to use up a lot of spirit/ Getting over it'. The boy helps the father return to the world, though understanding that part of him has died in the 'swampquakes of the slime of puddle soldiers'. He describes the whiteness of his father's body, his father's golden hair that he tenderly combs. In this poem too, there is laughter, only now it is the laughter of the survivor, so tainted by the horrors that have been experienced that it appears untrue. The final two lines focus on the laughing which appears deformed, ugly, joyless:

> A strange thing, with rickets – a hyena
> No singing – that kind of laughter.

(*CP* 754)

'For the Duration' explicitly sets his father's silence against the nightmares that return to haunt him and terrify the family:

> I could hear you from my bedroom –
> The whole hopelessness still going on,
> No-man's land still crying and burning
> Inside our house, and you climbing again
> Out of the trench, and wading back into the glare
>
> As if you might still not manage to reach us
> And carry us to safety.

(*CP* 761)

In this poem Hughes states bluntly that what most frightened him as a child was his father's refusal to talk about what had happened to him, so that the boy had to learn from other people's stories. Now, late in his own life, Hughes poses the fundamental question, the one he has always wanted to ask: 'Why couldn't I have borne/To hear you telling what you underwent?' He reasons that perhaps his father had not wanted to frighten him, but then turns that thought around, asking what it could have been that made his father's war more unbearable than anyone else's. Over time, he has 'fitted much of it together' – the award for gallantry his father received, the near-fatal wound – but he has never heard the stories from his father directly, and now it is too late and he never will. Keith Sagar suggests that in this poem, as in many of the war poems written around the same time, Hughes shows 'a new humility

and a deeper humanity'.[7] Certainly he returns again and again
to the same subject, exploring it in different ways, only now
focusing more on himself, on his own feelings and how his
father's silence has affected his subsequent life.

Hughes became Poet Laureate in December 1984, taking up
the position that John Betjeman had held since 1972. The role of
the Poet Laureate is to write occasional pieces for special events.
Hughes produced a poem to celebrate the birth of royal
children, birthday poems for the Queen, a poem on the fortieth
anniversary of the Queen's accession to the throne and one
particularly interesting long poem, entitled 'A Masque for Three
Voices', on the occasion of the Queen Mother's ninetieth
birthday in 1990. In an essay that appeared in *The Weekend
Telegraph* (4 August, 1990), Hughes discusses the thinking that
underpins the poem, and in so doing sets down his thoughts
about England and what it means to be British.

The essay starts with a conceit: if an epic dramatist were
writing a drama of the twentieth century, there would be two
main plots, one emerging from the Boer War (colonialism) and
the other from Russia (revolutionary Marxism that would lead
on to Stalin and the Cold War) with the Balkans as a sub-plot.
Since the Queen Mother was born at the start of the twentieth
century, her life-story spans the entire period, and in her
ninetieth year the Soviet system has finally collapsed. Hughes
proposes that his poem sees the period 'from the British point of
view', that is, from his own point of view, as 'the son of an
infantryman of the First World War.'[8] So crucial to that
perspective is the First World War that he refers to it as 'virtually
the Creation story'. Interestingly, he suggests that the war was
seen by many not as a victory but as a defeat, 'at least, it felt so in
the tribal lands of the north'. Grief for the generation that died
in the trenches was followed by the suffering of the Great
Depression, then by fears of a second war. Hughes writes that
long before 1939, he had a recurring dream about German
parachutists landing in the Calder Valley. This state of anxiety
had an effect on the mentality of the nation, he presents his
generation as born with a particular legacy:

> My historical horizon, typical for a great many of my generation, was
> closed by the dead of the First World War and the legend, beyond
> them, of the slavery of the nineteenth century in the great industrial

camps... One who was born of the First World War, who spent his first nine years dreaming of the Second, having lived through the Second went on well into his thirties expecting the nuclear Third and the chaos after.

This state of defensiveness helps to explain why the British have closed their minds to what he terms 'the great European intellectual debate' and why they have returned to a particular version of their 'sacred myth', which he sees as the Crown, embodied in the person of the Queen Mother.

The idea of the play underpins the poem, which is addressed to the Queen Mother. The three voices speak in heavily rhymed verse forms, the rhythms reflecting different fashions in dance music that are referred to through the poem. In the first section the notion of Britishness and the relationship between the individual and the idea of a nation is established:

> Being British is the mystery. Can you see
> That it is you or you or you or me?
> I do not understand how this can be.

> (CP 822)

Later, in the third section being British is linked to a history of conflict:

> Being British may be fact, faith, neither, or both.
> I only know what ghosts breathe in my breath –
> The shiver of their battles my Shibboleth.

> (CP 825)

The conflict of the Second World War transforms the king and queen into 'one sacred certainty that all can share', and in this situation, 'when man's future/Depended on one nation's soul', being British is no longer a mystery. The final section of the poem exalts the role of the Queen and the Queen Mother as the soul of the nation.

At first glance it might seem that the radical poet of *The Hawk in the Rain* has, over time, changed sides and has become firmly aligned with the Establishment. Yet if we look at the way in which Hughes's thinking about war, nation and community is reflected in his writing over more than three decades, the line of thought that equates Britishness with royalty as a sacred symbol is discernible. Hughes conceives of an England that has ancient roots in the soil, and when writing about his own birthplace in particular, he stresses that sense of continuity. He also depicts the inhabitants of the Calder Valley as archetypically English, resisting invaders, devising their own ways of coping with hardship, speaking their own version of the English language. These are the people who, in war-time, 'dreamed they thought they saw', as a new infant British nation, united in adversity, came into being.

Hughes ends his essay on the poem slightly defensively, however. He acknowledges that this way of seeing things is generational – 'as new generations begin to forget these things, meanings shifted'. The sentiments that had bound the nation together during the Second World War have lost their meaning. He wryly notes that one reader had complained that his poem was incomprehensible, despite his feeling that he had endeavoured to make it 'as accessible as possible'. The attitude to monarchy, to tradition, to a sense of community rooted in a particular place, to an idea of Britishness that emerged out of wartime experiences that Hughes acquired from his own life is also fading from memory. The generations following him have a different perspective.

One poem in *Remains of Elmet* hints at this great shift of perspective. 'Tick Tock Tick Tock' uses the story of Peter Pan, the boy who never grew up, to illustrate the gap between the poet's memories of 'the hills unalterable and the old women unalterable/ And the ageless boy' and a changing world. The Calder river flows past 'a hundred mill chimneys' as the boy plays in summer light, watching butterflies. But the clock ticks, and in the final lines the poet imagines himself swallowing that clock, and by its ticking sound bringing the fearsome crocodile that terrifies in *Peter Pan* crawling across the playground out of prehistory. The poem ends with this image: 'Tick tock tick tock the crocodile'. No one can remain a child forever, the world changes and the crocodile, whatever terrors it symbolises will come, drawn by the sound of time passing.

The tension between a changing world and the fixity of landscape runs right through Hughes's writing. He uses geological imagery to convey the idea of sedimented layers, of one world pressing down on another, burying earlier ones. In 'The Ancient Briton Lay under His Rock' he writes about himself as a boy, digging with his friends to try and find the long-dead mythical ancient hunter whose stories are still told in the valley. A poem in *Earth-Numb* (1979), 'Here is the Cathedral' is underpinned by the image of buried civilizations. A Roman bath house is being excavated from beneath the cathedral itself, and during the excavation, generations of other dead are emerging, the bones of people who died of plague, families buried together, now being picked over by archaeologists. Around the cathedral is tarmac, where lines of cars are parked. The contrast between the modern world and the ancient one is subtly drawn, with the string of images allowing readers to make their own connections. Then the mood changes: the focus of the poem shifts to an incident at the door of the cathedral. The poet gives some loose change to a grubby wino, then watches as he is evicted from the cathedral by a 'pink-scrubbed, brass-eyed Christian knight'. The message of the poem is plain: the coming of Christianity has done nothing to change man's basic brutality. The layers of dead being unearthed have nothing to say, except to reinforce the sad truth that cruelty and unkindness remain strong in the world.

It would be wrong to see Hughes's vision of humanity as unwaveringly bleak, however. Besides the imagery of geological and archaeological layers upon which new generations tread, is another image, that of genetic continuity. In 'For Billy Holt', in *Remains of Elmet*, traces of a Viking heritage can be seen 'anchored in nose and chin'. Earlier, in *Wodwo*, 'The Warriors of the North' sketches the coming of the Vikings and their gradual transformation into 'the iron arteries of Calvin'. The indomitable sense of resistance of the ancient Britons who held the Calder Valley against all comers and the savage strength of the Norsemen can be traced in the genetic fabric of the present. Other continuities are also observed. An uncollected poem about the poet's mother 'Edith' (*CP* 700) published in *The Listener* in 1985, depicts her walking over the moors as she approaches seventy, still dreaming dreams of freedom. She is described as a 'belated, errant, furious Brontë figment', and this conscious linking of Hughes's mother and a character from a Brontë novel continues a thread that is developed in *Remains of Elmet*, that of a literary continuity, a connection between writers across time. 'Top Withens', 'Haworth Parsonage', 'Emily Brontë' all develop the Brontë link, an obvious one in terms of simple geography, given the closeness of Haworth to Hughes's childhood home, and linked also to his relationship with Sylvia Plath, when the explicit comparison between Hughes and Heathcliffe had first been made. 'Wuthering Heights' in *Birthday Letters* brings all these threads together: the visit of Hughes and Plath to Yorkshire and their walk over the moors through Brontë country, the differences between what they each saw and how they responded, the difference between the fate of 'dour Emily' trapped in her small Yorkshire community and able only to leave it through her imagination and that of Sylvia Plath, bearer at that time of a 'huge/Mortgage of hope'. Looking back, he sees Plath through a series of photographic images, sitting in a tree, leaning against a stone wall. She is depicted as an elemental creature, the wind and the clouds come to look at her, even the grass 'took idiot notice of you'. The great promise of a brilliant future that Plath and Hughes shared when they first went to Yorkshire together is contrasted with the confined life of Emily Brontë, and the sadness of the loss of that promise pervades the poem. Just as the novel, *Wuthering Heights* ends with a description of the landscape, where possibly the ghosts of Heathcliffe and Cathy still walk, so this poem concludes with the same landscape, but with a hopeful final image: perhaps Emily's ghost, 'trying to hear your words' looked on, feeling a sudden surge of envy that is 'gradually quelled in understanding'. The fame of both women will endure, each of them in different ways as part of the landscape now.

One of the most memorable poems in *Remains of Elmet* is 'Heptonstall Cemetery'. In this short poem, Hughes lists the names of his beloved dead – Thomas, Walter, Edith, Esther and Sylvia, 'living feathers' on the wings of 'a family of dark swans' that fly on towards the Atlantic, towards the mythical Western lands. It is a beautiful imagist poem, that brings together the physical reality of the graves in the cemetery with the metamorphosis of the dead into birds. Significantly, these birds are not carrion-eaters, not crows, not savage birds, of the kind that peopled Hughes's earlier poetry, they are strong, lovely birds capable of beating through storm-clouds. Diane Middlebrook sees this poem as important, suggesting that the inclusion of Plath's name indicates a process that he was going through as he worked on editing her poems, journals and stories for publication:

> Gradually, he was drawing his mother and Sylvia Plath together as composite influences in the history of his vocation.[9]

The mystery of being British and what that might signify to him is continually being explored by Ted Hughes. He articulates his sense of identity in different ways – through the enduring nature of the land, both the Yorkshire of his youth and the Devon of his later years, through its stones, grass, and soil, through the layers of civilization that are buried in the earth, through the genetic continuity that is still discernible in the faces of ordinary men and women, through shared memories, through history, whether ancient or more recent, a history of religion, conflict, pain and survival, through the connections between writers, through story-telling, through symbolic associations. *Remains of Elmet* may not be one of Hughes's best-known collections, but it is significant, for it brings together many of the themes he had been exploring earlier in his writing, and through its elegiac quality establishes other themes that he would follow later.

# 4

'His voice felt out of the way. "I am", he said': Language and Mythology

Throughout his writing life, Ted Hughes experimented with different forms, going beyond poetry to work with both prose and play-writing. Sometimes his experiments were well-received by critics, at other times less so, and some of his work aroused strong conflicting opinions. *Gaudete,* for instance, has been hailed as a masterpiece by some, and condemned as 'a ludicrous travesty' by Anthony Thwaite, who describes Hughes as a fascinating but often bewildering writer.[1] What links all his writing, however, no matter whether he was producing poetry, stories, plays, translations or critical studies are his constant endeavours to push the boundaries of language, to test the elasticity of English and to use all kinds of different registers, from high poetic language to colloquial Yorkshire speech. Writing in different genres enabled him to try out varieties of English, and his work for the theatre and stories for children reflect a growing interest in orality.

There is also another element that connects Hughes's writing over several decades: the recurrent presence of two mythical figures, one male and one female, who came to occupy a central place in his thinking and who emerge again and again in diverse ways in his works. The first of these is the Great Goddess, a figure of universal power, whose presence is strongly evident in Celtic mythology.

When Hughes went up to Cambridge in 1951 to read English, his teacher gave him a copy of Robert Graves's *The White Goddess* as a gift. This work was something of a cult book among English

65

literature students at the time, and he introduced Sylvia Plath to it, with extraordinary results. Graves's hypothesis is that the oldest form of religion is worship of the moon goddess in her three phases: the waxing moon is a young, beautiful woman, whose colour is white, the full moon is the sensual, strong, maternal woman whose colour is red, the waning moon is a hag, whose task is to lay out the dead and whose colour is black. In the ancient world the goddess was all-powerful, until deposed by male-centred religions such as Christianity, where she survives as one manifestation in the figure of the Virgin Mary. Part of the ritual worship of the goddess according to Graves involved the creation of poetry:

> Poetry began in the matriarchal age, and derives its magic from the moon, not from the sun. No poet can hope to understand the nature of poetry unless he has had a vision of the Naked King crucified to the lopped oak, and watched the dancers, red-eyed from the acrid smoke of sacrificial fires, stamping out the measure of the dance, their bodies bent uncouthly forward, with a monotonous chant of 'Kill! Kill ! Kill!' and 'Blood! Blood! Blood!' [2]

Poetry has its origins in blood-sacrifice to the goddess, and in worshipping her the poet discovers his muse. The goddess is all-giving and all-devouring, she is the sow that eats her own young, the crone picking over dead bodies on the battlefield, the life-giving mother and the sexual predator. Graves poses the question as to the use or function of poetry in the modern world, and answers himself in a way that would have had strong appeal to the young Hughes:

> The function of poetry is religious invocation of the Muse; its use is the experience of mixed exaltation and horror that her presence excites.[3]

Plath incorporated this triple dimension into her poetic vision, as does Hughes, though differently. For Graves's vision is essentially male-centred, woman is muse not poet in her own right. Plath took the idea of the goddess and transformed it into a woman-centred myth; Hughes's struggles with female sexuality as demonstrated in poetry from what has been termed his middle period, including works such as *Crow* and most especially *Gaudete* show him endeavouring, in Graves's terms, to accommodate the goddess into his life. The destructive power of sexuality that is so evident in *Crow* is replaced in later work by a female symbolism that focuses more on the maternal, both human and animal, but the role of the goddess in the creation of poetry is fundamental. Responding to critics accusing him of celebrating violence in poems like 'Hawk Roosting' and 'The Jaguar', Hughes states that he thinks of such poems as 'invocations of the goddess'. The importance of the goddess figure in his work is well-summed up by Gifford and Roberts, who argue that Hughes has been most consistently inspired by this myth:

> The goddess is implicit in his work from the beginning, but becomes increasingly prominent, in the 'mother'of several of the *Crow* poems, in the object of Lumb's devotion in *Gaudete*, and in the hero's victim and bride in *Cave Birds*. The rational and moral controlling consciousness's dealings with her are the theme of Hughes' synoptic interpretation of Shakespeare in *A Choice of Shakespeare's Verse*. The goddess is not separate from the world of things, and she is present also in the human unconscious, accessible to disciplined techniques of imagination, states of meditation, ecstasy, extremes of anguish or of bliss.[4]

The second significant mythical figure is Prometheus, hero of ancient Greek myth. The legend of Prometheus is a powerful one: one of the last of the Titans, Prometheus had the gift of foresight. After Zeus crushed the Titans, Prometheus refused to bow down to the new god. One version of the legend has Prometheus as the creator of mankind, which he fashioned out of earth and water, and into whom the goddess Athene then breathed soul and life. What all versions of the Prometheus story relate is that he stole fire from the gods for use by human beings, and was punished by being chained to a rock, where savage birds, in some versions a lone vulture, tore out his liver afresh every day. How long he was tortured like this also varies, in some versions for thousands of years, but Prometheus was eventually released by Hercules, Zeus having relented. Eventually he was admitted to the home of the gods on Mount Olympus and was worshipped as protector of arts and sciences, since he is said to have given mankind words and numbers. It is not difficult to see why this myth should have held particular appeal for Hughes, and in some respects the story of Crow can be seen as a variation on the Prometheus story. Crow is the trickster, one who, like Prometheus, challenges authority, one who dares, who suffers, who is tormented. Both Crow and Prometheus challenge the gods and are punished for their daring.

Ultimately, through the power of his own words (Zeus relents when Prometheus foretells his downfall, thereby enabling him to act in order to avoid it and so change his destiny) Prometheus is released. The torments he endured are finally eased through his skilful use of language. The connection between creativity and Prometheus, stealer of fire is self-evident, a connection that Hughes found fascinating. Keith Sagar suggests that in the early 1970s Hughes was wrestling with several versions of the Prometheus story in his writing, possibly without realizing it at first. In *Orghast, Prometheus on his Crag, Gaudete, Cave Birds* and *Adam and the Sacred Nine* Hughes explores versions of the same myth, a story of conflict raging in an individual who is unable to reconcile his mortal and immortal natures.[5] Hughes the writer and Hughes the grief-stricken man could find a reflection in the story of Prometheus's suffering.

Both the Prometheus and the Great Goddess myths are, therefore, in different ways, narratives about language and creativity. In his reviews and prefaces to the work of other poets, Hughes writes about what poetry means to him, returning again and again to its transformative powers, and to the cost of being a poet in terms of personal suffering and artistic striving. The process of becoming a poet is a mysterious one, and once the vocation has begun, the role of the poet is to keep faith with oneself and to pursue the instructions of the goddess. The opacity of the demands she makes upon her acolytes means that poets struggle to make sense of what they do and in that struggle, many do not follow their calling to extremes. In his preface to his anthology of Shakespeare's verse, published in 1971, Hughes discusses the complexity of being a poet:

> It might be said – every poet does no more than find metaphors for his own nature. That would be only partly true. Most poets never come anywhere near devining the master-plan of their whole make-up and projecting it complete. The majority cling to some favoured corner of it, or to remotely transmitted Reuter-like despatches, or mistranslate its signals into the language of a false nature.[6]

Hughes can hardly be said to be a writer clinging to some favoured corner; rather he has constantly experimented, trying out new ideas and working methods, with his two basic myths as the corner-stones. Implicit in his theories about the role of the poet is a sense of the poet's specialness; like a shaman, a true poet is marked out in some way from the rest of society.

In 1992, Hughes published a monograph on Shakespeare. *Shakespeare and the Goddess of Complete Being* is, in many respects, a study not only of Shakespeare but of Hughes's theory of the central significance of the goddess for all great writers. The book develops ideas he had expounded in his edition of Shakespeare's verse some twenty years earlier, and shows how central Shakespeare was to his ideas about the role and function of the poet. Hughes's contention is that there is a fundamental structural pattern which recurs in Shakespeare's mature plays, starting with *All's Well that Ends Well,* a pattern which he terms Shakespeare's 'equation'. This equation can be traced to two early works, often marginalized by critics, *Venus and Adonis* and *The Rape of Lucrece.* Each of these poems incorporates one of the two fundamental myths of the equation, myths which Hughes sees as linked to the history of sixteenth century religion in England. The myth of Venus and Adonis, which tells the story of the passion of the goddess for Adonis, who dies violently and is resurrected by her and carried into heaven is for Hughes the basic myth of Catholicism. The story of Tarquin's rape of Lucrece and his subsequent punishment when she kills herself is the myth that lies behind Puritan attitudes to sexuality and derives from ancient myths about the conflict between male and female gods. Hughes suggests that Shakespeare worked with these two myths from the ancient world, incorporating them in different ways into his plays and so effectively writing the story of the religious conflicts of his own time. Hughes spent several years working on the book, and though it was not favourably received by critics and was seen by some as obsessive and idiosyncratic, it nevertheless should be taken as a serious statement about the connection between goddess worship and creativity in Hughes's personal universe.

Shakespeare was, for Hughes, a shaman of his time, a writer who received a visitation 'from the other side'. Hughes elaborates on why figures such as Shakespeare, T.S. Eliot and

Yeats emerge at certain historical moments, noting that great shamans appear when a society is in a time of crisis:

> Throughout history, as countless precedents show, wherever a people, or a culture, or a social group, is threatened either with extinction of ultimate persecution and assimilation by the enemy, the great shaman tends to appear. The lesser shamans heal and solve problems with transcendental help. The great shaman, typically, gathers up the whole tradition of the despairing group, especially the very earliest mythic/religious traditions with all the circumstances of their present sufferings, into a messianic, healing, redemptive vision on the spiritual plane.[7]

The key words here are 'healing', 'redemptive' and 'messianic.' The shaman's task, like that of the exceptional poet, is to seek his own redemption and, through his suffering, the redemption of the wider group. The poet acquires huge symbolic importance in Hughes's vision, as a being who can be in touch with past and present, with the real world and an alternative one, and through this unique relationship can bring healing. Dennis Walder suggests that Hughes has an exalted conception of the role of the poet in society:

> He feels that by exploring his own imagination, he is exploring everyone's; he is the poet as bard, as singer of the community's songs, expressing itself to itself, defining its real identity.[8]

This conception of the poet's role is bound up with both goddess worship and the Prometheus myth. Hughes constantly transforms the basic components of his own life into myth, and the narrative of his quest for redemption runs through his writing and can be traced also in his attempts to redefine poetic language.

1971 was an important year for Hughes, in terms of his development as a writer. His Shakespeare anthology appeared, and later the ideas articulated in his preface would turn into the monograph, he was still writing more Crow poems, editing Plath's poetry for publication, and his play, *Orpheus* was premiered on BBC radio. Most significant of all, however, was his collaboration with Peter Brook, with whom he travelled to Persia for the performance of *Orghast* at a theatre festival in Persepolis. Working with Brook suited Hughes; he was not interested in the theatre as a vehicle primarily for playwrights, a view which separated him from the mainstream trend of that time, for since the late 1950s with the emergence of playwrights like John Osborne and Arnold Wesker, the British theatre had been dominated by writers. Brook's method of working, which involved lengthy periods of improvisation and the forming of actors into an ensemble was congenial to Hughes. In *Orghast* the intention was to explore the Prometheus myth in new ways. The programme note set out a series of questions that the production planned to explore:

> What is the relation between verbal and non-verbal theatre? What happens when gesture and sound turn into word? What is the exact place of the word in theatrical expression? As vibration? Concept? Music? Is any evidence buried in the sound structure of certain ancient languages?[9]

Hughes's task was to create a new language, and in a radio interview with Stan Correy and Robyn Ravlich in 1982, he explains the working process he undertook with Brook. The idea was to put on a performance based on different texts, including *Prometheus Bound,* Calderon's *Life is Dream* and early Persian religious texts. There was no single story at the centre, so writer and director had to create a series of scenes. Hughes explains how the original idea was to have something like an opera, with 'nothing comprehensible linguistically at all', the sense emerging out of the situations devised with the actors.[10] Hughes came to feel dissatisfied with the early attempts that drew on existing ancient languages, and began to invent a language of his own. Since the basic idea was the story of Prometheus and the vulture, he started with Brook's central image, which was fire, inventing a word for fire, then a word for sun, then a series of other words:

> I could then develop a whole language by a sort of metaphorical process – of making bundles of the sounds that composed these other ideas, so that any particular word I needed in my text, I could fit together out of the sounds that I already had.

Eventually, he started writing just in sounds, composing each scene and working with the actors who used the sounds as a basis for their improvisation.

Asked about the contrast between creating something like *Orghast* and writing in everyday language, Hughes responded by arguing that they were not so far apart, since *Orghast* was an

71

experiment in stripping away the intrusive, more formal aspects of language and endeavouring to find a way of signalling how people actually communicate with one another and how rich ordinary conversation can be:

> And it's that richness that we tried to draw on in *Orghast,* and it's that richness that you're always trying to get back to when you say: 'We must write ordinary speech. We must use the speech that we do use, that we ordinarily *do* use, because that's the only living speech.'

Through his linguistic experiments, Hughes found himself being led full circle back to living speech, to the language in daily use, the kind of language that he had always seen as an important link in an historical chain. This process of developing understanding and shifting his ideas about language suggests that working on *Orghast* was a transformative experience for Hughes. The importance of the collaboration with Brook on this project in terms of Hughes's subsequent development has not been as fully recognized as it deserves to be. The Orghast experiment enabled Hughes to engage with several lines of thought that had been growing in significance for him. Firstly, most obviously, was further exploration of the Prometheus myth; secondly, the unique opportunity to invent a language led to a profound discovery about the importance of orality and the richness of ordinary speech. The deeper he went into language, he told A.C. Smith who was documenting the production process, 'the less visual/conceptual its imagery, and the more audial/visceral/muscular its system of tensions'.[11] Hughes had always written in very strongly stressed language, but after this experience he came to a deeper understanding of what exactly he wanted language to do. Thirdly, *Orghast* offered Hughes a means of pulling together his two great foundation myths, the myth of the goddess and the myth of Prometheus, as he explains, again to Smith:

> Part I is the story of the crime against material nature, the creatress, source of life and light, by the violater, the mental tyrant Holdfast, and her revenge. The first plan of her revenge is on the animal level, and it fails...the second plan is on the truly human level, and it succeeds, transcending the conflict by creating a being which, like Prometheus (this is the story of how he survives) includes the elemental opposites, and in whom the collision and pain become illumination.[12]

In the second part of the performance, the vulture that has tortured Prometheus, which is killed by Hercules in the original myth, is transformed into a woman, into the supreme goddess herself, in a process of reconciliation. Out of pain and suffering comes hope and a sense of meaningfulness.

While working on *Orghast*, Hughes wrote a sequence of poems, twenty-one of which were collected and published in 1973 as *Prometheus on His Crag*. When he brought out *Moortown* in 1979, he decided to include these Prometheus poems, with three omitted and three new ones, along with another sequence about a fallen man, the biblical Adam and some of the poems from *Orts* (1978) renamed here as *Earth-Numb*. One can only speculate that part of his thinking about the *Moortown* volume was a desire to show the new range of poetic voices that he had at his command, which included both some of his best elegiac nature writing, as was discussed in chapter 3, and poems produced at different stages in his career which are completely different in tone and language. Sagar suggests that Hughes's ordering of the sections of *Moortown* were designed to show a move from earth-bound suffering through numbness to rebirth, but though this may be feasible in thematic terms, the variety of language that the poems in this collection reveal must also have been a contributory factor to his decision to include such diverse sequences in a single volume.

Stuart Hirschberg, in his book on Hughes's use of myth, suggests that by writing about Prometheus Hughes was struggling with a profound dichotomy within himself towards what Hirschberg calls 'the sources of feminine nurturing'.[13] The mother is another aspect of the goddess, a savage figure who cannot prevent the torments that her son must endure. As Hughes explored ideas of redemption, he nevertheless kept returning to the idea of the scapegoat, the sacrificial victim who must suffer and possibly die before reconciliation is possible. Interestingly, what is missing from Hughes's mythical universe is the gentle maternal model of the Christian mother, the Virgin Mary who mourns her lost Son. Birth in Hughes's universe means pain for the mother and the beginning of another kind of pain for the new human creature. Giving birth to Prometheus in her agony, 'His mother covers her eyes'.

What the sequence of Prometheus poems shows, however, is Prometheus slowly coming to terms with his own suffering and

73

in the final poem being reborn into a new dimension, where he 'treads/On the dusty peacock film where the world floats'. There is no solution proposed here, no promise of better things to come, but there is a definite sense that his agony has come to an end. What he will do now, what words he will use to communicate in this new state of being remains unknown. As he 'eases free', the images are all about his movements, not his voice: he sways, balances, then treads. Like a small child he has taken his first tentative step.

The first poem in the Prometheus cycle opens with the protagonist struggling to find a voice. The opening line consists of two statements: 'His voice felt out of the way. "I am", he said'. Prometheus is disconnected from his own power of speech, he has a voice, but is not in control of it, it feels 'out of the way'. Later in the poem, he is depicted as having a 'mouth-mask.' The phrase 'I am', with its Biblical resonances appears to be one of self-assertion, but this is undercut in the next two lines as the statement turns into a longer, more ambiguous sentence:

> 'Returning,' he said, and 'Now I am
> Feeling into my body', and 'Something is strange –
>
> (CP 285)

Prometheus is coming in to consciousness, unclear about who or what he is. His final question is simply 'Am I an eagle?' as he no longer knows who or what he is, whether he is a man or a Titan. Only by poem 18 does revelation start to come, when a tiny lizard whispers in his ear even as the vulture tears out his entrails, 'Lucky, you are so lucky to be human'.

In the second poem he is starting to wake up to his surroundings, feeling like an eagle as his strength flows back into him, but this power is short-lived, for by the third poem his torment is about to begin as the vulture awakens and 'a world of holy, happy notions shattered', while he is pestered by birds, here depicted as noisy, savage creatures, 'scratching, probing, peering for a lost world'.

Poem 4, one of the shortest, depicts Prometheus watching the vulture coming out of the sun, watching it as it splits him open, able only 'to peruse its feathers' each of which tells him the same thing:

> 'Today is a fresh start
> Torn up by its roots
> As I tear the liver from your body'

(CP 287)

In his suffering, Prometheus is at first paralysed, then slowly comes to admire the vulture which can not only carry out its daily task but manages 'also to digest its guilt'. Slowly Prometheus starts to reflect on what the vulture signifies. He begins by thinking of the vulture as 'the revenge of the wombs', since he had stolen the holy fire and hidden it in them. By poem 20, as he thinks about the vulture, he asks a string of questions to which he can find no answers – is it his own 'unborn half-self', is it 'his prophetic familiar', is it the fire he stole, is it atomic law, is it 'the earth's enlightenment', is it his 'anti-self' coming to pull him into unbeing? The final question that drifts into his mind, circling as the vulture circles gives a glimmer of hope:

> Or was it, after all, the Helper
> Coming again to pick at the crucial knot
> Of all his bonds...?

(CP 296)

The Prometheus myth is treated in a different way in another sequence of poems that was published by Rainbow Press in 1970, then also included, with some revisions in *Moortown*. *Adam and the Sacred Nine* is a sequence of poems about Adam who is visited by nine birds, as he lies prostrate in a state of despair. Like Prometheus, Adam is cut off from the world, though there is no hint in these poems as to how that has happened and, significantly, there is no reference to Eve. Adam has shrunk back into himself, ignoring the calls of living creatures around him, urging him to wake up and take up his rightful place in the world. A disembodied thing, Adam's skeleton 'glittered in its hangar of emptiness./ Like the Southern Cross'. His suffering is different from that of Prometheus, he is not physically tortured, his is an existential pain – 'his cry/Was sun-grief', 'his cry was random atoms'. The birds who come to him do not come to add to his torment, as the vulture does to Prometheus, they come bringing messages about what it means to be alive. Each bird embodies a particular quality. First to visit Adam is the Falcon, the bird of prey, driven by desire to hunt and kill,

75

With the bullet-brow
Of burying himself head-first and ahead
Of his delicate bones, into the target
Collision.

(CP 445)

Then comes the ultimate songbird, the Skylark, 'thatching the sun with bird-joy', followed by the nurturing warmth of the Wild Duck, the speed and power of the Swift, the strength of the tiny Wren, the Owl, 'a masked soul listening for death', the female Dove, 'her breast big with rainbows'. The birds in different ways symbolize aspects of life, both creative and destructive, nurturing and harming. When Crow finally comes, whispering secrets in Adam's ear, Adam wakes. Then comes the final visitation, the Phoenix, the magical bird that is consumed by fire and dying, is reborn into new life:

Where it descends
Where it offers itself up

And naked the newborn
Laughs in the blaze

(CP 450)

After the Phoenix's laughter, Adam begins to stir, and in the poem 'Light' he opens his eyes and sees leaves, while 'Light smiled/ And smiled and smiled'. The final two poems of the sequence can be read as kind of creation story. In 'Bud-tipped twig' Adam and the world itself discover touch: the protagonist of this poem is a disembodied breast that lifts 'its simple face/To the sun'. Touch is at first terrifying: a tree recoils from it, the grass shrinks from it, even brambles that touch by chance spring away. Clouds above spread coldness over the breast, the sea with is own preoccupations 'made the breast feel lost'. But the breast looks up at the sun, unable to see or hear or cry, and the implication here is that nature, existence must be accepted for what it is. There is not necessarily any connection to be made through touching, but touching is an essential part of being alive. The final poem, 'The sole of a foot' is more explicitly affirmative. As the sole of a foot is pressed against rock, man taking his first steps in the world, the short poem is filled with words that have positive connotations: 'warm, comfortable,

76

gladdened, gentle, grateful'. In the final lines, the sole of the foot speaks, affirming its role in the world:

> I am no wing
> To tread emptiness.
> I was made
>
> For you.

(CP 452)

Curiously, both these final poems were left out when the sequence was published in *Moortown*, which left 'Light' as the end poem, with its more cynical last lines: as Adam opens his eyes and light smiles at him, he is suddenly gripped by fear:

> Afraid suddenly
> That this was all there was to it.

(CP 451)

These two very different endings to *Adam and the Sacred Nine* are a good illustration of the way in which Hughes could rethink his own work, altering the mood and the message by a subtle process of editing. The ending in the Moortown version is closer to the mood of *Crow*.

The fourth section of *Moortown, Earth-Numb* contains another sequence of poems about a suffering individual who is disconnected from the world and struggling to find some form of redemption. *Seven Dungeon Songs* opens with a poem about origins, in which a wounded wolf runs through the stars with a new born baby. The nurturing wolf, an archetypal mythical creature, suffers pain in this poem, and even as its milk drips, so also does its blood. Man comes into a world of suffering, born 'soft-brained' and not yet aware of this. In the last two lines some awareness is starting, as 'the baby's cry/Echoed among the precipices'.

The second poem recounts the destruction of the mother goddess by a male god, who is 'himself nothing'. That god may or may not be the protagonist of the third poem, the I-speaker who is assembling himself, putting together face, hands, shoulders, legs and making himself a body. But even having assembled himself, the narrator cannot move, and the fourth poem sees him lying 'like the already-dead', in a world where light has been locked out. The frantic pointless activity of the narrator in the fifth poem gives way to the silence of the sixth, where

> The eyes of the witnesses,
> The human eyes, jammed in flesh,
> Which seemed to know, in their silence,
> Were graves
> Of silence.
>
> (*CP* 562)

The final poem is all in the conditional, with eleven lines out of sixteen beginning with the word 'if'. The human body and the earth are fused into one in an extraordinary series of apocalyptic images: 'if mouth could open its cliff', 'if skin of grass could take messages', 'if spine of earth-foetus/Could unfurl'. If all these conditions were to be met, then as the last two lines tell us, 'The speech that works air/Might speak me'. The imprisoned narrator understands that language can free him, but for that to happen, man and nature must come together in a mystical union that will bring about rebirth. The liberation is still only longed for, still only a dream or a hope, but at least that hope is being expressed.

Some critics, notably Keith Sagar who knew Hughes well, have analysed his poetry in terms of a personal journey from great pain to a position of acceptance and greater quietness. Sagar sees Hughes's collection *River,* published in 1983, as marking 'the end of his poetic journey, from a world made of blood to a world made of light.'[14] It is the case that in the 1980s Hughes's intense interest in the Prometheus myth and in exploring aspects of suffering and redemption started to change and he returned to writing about the natural world, to making poems about birds, fish, flowers and landscape. *River* is an interesting collection, since it not only illustrates his lifelong passion for fishing, but it also contains poems written about other places than his native Yorkshire, a sign that Hughes was drawing upon new experiences and images. In a note to 'That Morning', Hughes points out that the river in the poem is in Alaska, then he goes on to recall a childhood memory of wartime England, when waves of Lancaster bombers flew overhead. The poem brings together that memory with the beauty of watching wild salmon moving upstream and seeing bears come down to the water's edge to catch the fish. The poem concludes with three lines that Sagar has taken as the basis for his interpretation:

> So we found the end of our journey.
>
> So we stood, alive in the river of light
> Among the creatures of light, creatures of light.

*(CP 664)*

Undeniably, there is a change of mood in much of the poetry from the early 1980s onwards, but attempts to fit Hughes's writing neatly into categories or to identify precise shifts of position need to take account of the broader picture. Hughes certainly did experiment with some very dark material in the traumatic period after the deaths of Sylvia Plath and Assia Weevil, but there were many other factors affecting his writing and influencing his thinking. What he seems to have been primarily trying to do was to find a way of exploring the role of poetry in a world turned dark, and it is significant that he read so much work by writers from other countries who had endured great suffering and yet continued to produce poetry. Moreover, in his experiments with language, Hughes was continually trying out different ways of writing. One line of writing that he continued to produce steadily led to poetry, stories and plays for children.

Already, back in 1968, Hughes had written what was to be one of his best-known works, a children's fable entitled *The Iron Man* and he continued to write for children even while working through some of his most despairing images in his adult poetry. *The Coming of the Kings,* for example, is a nativity play, that satirizes greed and social injustice. The fat priest, the venal innkeeper and his wife, the police inspector are all oblivious to what is happening around them; only the minstrel can see the movement of a strange star in the heavens. The others are all preparing for the arrival of three great kings, and the innkeeper turns Mary and Joseph away because the rooms are to be given to greater people than they are. When the kings arrive, they go straight to the stable, ignoring both the inn and the innkeeper, the personification of human ignorance, who is left complaining that he does not know what is going on:

Who's been born? What's happening?
Why are the three great kings going into my old stable?
Why is that star standing over the roof of my old stable?
Who has lit that great light inside my old stable?

The last words, significantly, go to the minstrel, in a speech about falling snow. 'Every snowflake is an angel', the minstrel proclaims, 'the world will be deep in angels'. This play, along with three others for children was published in 1970, the year that saw the publication of *Crow*.

*The Iron Man* is also a fable about human ignorance, or rather about adult ignorance, for the world is eventually saved by a child. A strange man of iron appears one day, and starts to eat everything he can find that is made of metal. One small boy, Hogarth, sees this Iron Man, and agrees to help angry farmers who have lost all their machinery to trap him in a pit. The Iron Man is caught and buried under tons of earth. Hogarth feels some remorse, but the world has returned to normality. Then, in the Spring, the Iron Man rises up out of the ground, and it is now up to Hogarth to apologize to him and to suggest a way for everyone to live together: the Iron Man is led to a scrapyard where he can eat all the metal he wants.

This new-found trust between humans and giant concludes the first part of the story. In the second part another creature appears, a space dragon that wants to eat living things. Human weapons cannot deter the monster, so Hogarth appeals to the Iron Man who challenges the dragon to fight. The Iron Man defeats the dragon, who is sent back into space to make beautiful music which gradually changes the minds of human beings, who stop manufacturing weapons and live in peace with one another.

The appeal of the fable is twofold – on the one hand, the archetypal ingredients are all present – savage creatures tamed, the central role of a small boy who is wiser than adults, the clash between monsters and the final resolution. On the other hand, it is also a fable about the modern world, one where scrap yards, rotting metal and weapons proliferate until overcome by the power of musical harmony. That Hughes could write such works while also working with the story of Crow and developing his ideas about Prometheus shows the breadth of his talent as a writer. There is much more to Hughes than poetry of violence and despair, and in reading his work holistically, it is important to set the terrible deaths of two of the women he loved into a wider context. Worship of the goddess could indeed lead to torment and madness, but there is also the promise of redemption through suffering and the need to acknowledge the power of looking at the world through the eyes of a child. Writing for children enabled him to engage with childhood perception, untainted by adult suffering and rationality. Prometheus learns to see again, he is restored through language, and it is through speaking to the Iron Man that the child saves the world. The title poem, 'The River' opens with a pietà, with the image of the river fallen from heaven, lying 'across/The lap of his mother, broken by the world', but then this image is immediately countered by the next two affirmative lines: 'But water will go on/issuing from heaven'. Experimenting with language, writing in different registers and for different audiences, endeavouring to invent a new language entirely enabled Hughes to move from a position where his voice felt out of the way, to a place where he could communicate with a increasing variety of readers of all ages with confidence.

# 5

## 'With the Word burn the hearts of the people': Ted Hughes and Translation

One major source of inspiration for Hughes, as he sought to expand his poetic repertoire, was the work of poets from other eras and other cultures, some of whom he read through translations. He was also a gifted translator himself, both of poetry and drama, ancient and modern; translating enabled him to expand and innovate, as well as ensuring the continuity of great writing from the past. Hughes was by no means an insular poet, and believed that the role of the writer was to create his own poetry but at the same time to acknowledge what he inherited from writers who had preceded him.

Hughes can be seen as a natural born translator, who always sought to 'translate' the language of his Yorkshire origins into poetry. Discussing his work, Seamus Heaney stresses Hughes's Englishness and his debt to the great alliterative tradition of English poetry, drawing attention to the crucial importance of language combinations in his own writing:

> What Hughes alone could write depended for its release on the discovery of a way to undam the energies of the dialect, to get a stomping ground for that inner freedom, to get that childhood self a disguise to roam at large in. Freedom and naturalness and home-liness are positives in Hughes' critical vocabulary, and they are linked with both the authenticity of individual poets and the genius of the language itself.[1]

As was noted in the last chapter, Hughes drew upon a huge variety of different sources and wrote for different kinds of readership, which by implication involves processes that can effectively be termed translational. The shaman, in Hughes's vision, is also a translator, someone who crosses over into another dimension, then brings back news of his experiences in a form that is accessible to the people waiting for his message. Translation is therefore a key concept in understanding Hughes's work, and it is significant that as he grew older, his translating became even more important to him.

Translation has not been well served by literary critics, who have often seen this type of literary practice as a secondary form of writing, a second-class art that lacks originality. The prevalence of this view has led to an undervaluation of the role translation plays in the development of any national literature, and of the importance that translation may have in the development of an individual writer. However, research in the newly established discipline of translation studies has shown that translation is one of the greatest shaping forces in the history of literature, and periods of great literary activity are usually preceded by periods of intensive translation. So, for example, the English Renaissance was preceded by a century of translation from ancient and contemporary European languages, a century dominated by huge international debates about the translation of sacred works, in particular the Bible. When Shakespeare came to write, the sonnet had become an established English poetic form and he had at his disposal a huge body of work translated from Latin, Italian and French upon which he drew for the construction of many of his plays. For T.S. Eliot and Yeats, both writers that Hughes admired, translation was also crucially important, as indeed it was for so many others. Alexander Pope may be remembered today primarily as a satirist, but in his own time he was renowned as one of the greatest translators of Homer. The down-grading of translation distorts its importance as a source of innovation and renewal for writers through the ages.

Through translation writers can access works produced in other cultures and at other moments in time, and so expand their own poetic universe. It may be that a writer is particularly drawn to another writer, or to particular works, as Seamus Heaney is drawn to *The Divine Comedy*, for example, or as Ezra Pound was drawn to classical Chinese poetry. In cases of empathy between writer and translation, the act of translating becomes in effect a logical next step in that writer's literary development. This would seem to be the case with Hughes's translation of Seneca's *Oedipus*, which was commissioned by Peter Brook for a production starring John Gielgud and Irene Worth, who Hughes admired greatly, at the National Theatre in 1968. Originally, the translation had been commissioned from David Turner for a production to be directed by Sir Lawrence Olivier, but Olivier became ill, and when Brook took over he wanted a different version, so Turner was replaced as translator. Hughes came in at very short notice, and in his generous tribute to Hughes in the published version, Turner acknowledges the extraordinariness of Hughes's achievement:

> Three weeks later when the nucleus of the production assembled to hear some of Ted's first rough jottings, it was obvious from the moment he spoke that improvement was too weak a word for what he had done. It was more like an apotheosis. In place of good serviceable prose there was inspiration, elegance, fire, poetry. It was all magic. And all the magic was Ted's.[2]

In the preface to his translation, Hughes explains how he was writing specifically for Brook's company, adding little but deleting a lot. In an interview with Ekbert Faas he expands on this, and explains how important this translation was as an influence on the rest of his writing. The simplicity of the Oedipus story in Seneca's pared-down rendering of it, he believed, led him to focus very sharply on the kind of language he needed to use. Having produced one draft, he felt that the language was 'too light', so produced subsequent drafts:

> And as I worked on it, it turned into a process of more and more simplifying, or in a way limiting the language. I ended up with something like three hundred words, the smallest vocabulary Gielgud had ever worked with. And that ran straight into *Crow*. However, it was a way of concentrating my actual writing rather than of bringing me to any language that was then useful in *Crow*. It simply concentrated me.[3]

The language Hughes uses in *Oedipus* is very concentrated, and the play is not in any way Latinate. The characters use very plain language, speaking in short, staccato phrases. Hughes deliberately uses a system of spaces between words and phrases rather than conventional punctuation as in this passage, with

Oedipus speaking his final words as he leaves the stage:

> The contagion is leaving your land am taking it with me
>     I am taking it away          fate          remorseless my
> enemy      you are the friend I choose          come with me
>           pestilence          ulcerous agony          blasting
> consumption          plague terror          plague blackness
>      despair      welcome          come with me          you
> are my guides      lead me

Hughes used translation instrumentally, focusing his mind on what to do in his own language with a work written by someone else.

In his collection of poems written in memory of Hughes, *Letters to Ted*, Daniel Weissbort contrasts Hughes's translations of plays with some of his other translations:

> The plays you translated you made something of,
> Your translations of the verse of friends comparatively
>                                             little ...
> ... As for your 'X-ray vision'. . .
> You were attacked on account of it, for being too literal,
> In that you told no more than you saw or heard,
> Keeping your eye on the task, not yourself.
> Still, the words *were* yours.[4]

Weissbort's notes to this poem and to another entitled 'A Translation' are revealing in what they tell us about Hughes's translation practice. Weissbort suggests that Hughes felt much freer when working with theatre texts, whereas at other times, with poetry, he felt constrained by the original, often following word order and syntax quite literally. He believes that Hughes worked best when dealing with 'the rawest raw material', ideally with literal or partial translations that he could then rework. Weissbort's view is that Hughes could not start translating properly until 'he had the sense of having seen through to the centre of the poem, to its inspiration'.[5] What mattered to Hughes in translating was to go back in some way to the source, a technique very similar to that of Ezra Pound who, in his essay on Cavalcanti, admitted that when he first started to translate the Italian poet he had not actually touched the essence of his work at all, having been caught in two linguistic traps: the difficulty of Cavalcanti's Italian and the dead weight of Victorian English. Hughes similarly worked by stripping down what he saw as excessive linguistic layers, shortening and tightening as he rewrote.

The reference to Hughes's 'X-ray vision' comes from notes written by the Hungarian co-translator with whom he collaborated on English versions of the poetry of János Pilinszky. János Csokits explains in his essay that Hughes did not want to create smooth, polished English renderings and that in his first, literal drafts he tried to retain some sense of the original syntax to help Hughes reshape the poems into their English versions. However, he attributes to Hughes a capacity for grasping the quality, style and characteristics of a poem even in a basic word-for-word translation:

> It is almost as if he could X-ray the literals and see the original poem in ghostly detail like a radiologist viewing the bones, muscles, veins and nerves of a live human body...The effect is not that of a technical device; it has more to do with extra-sensory perception.[6]

In his introduction to a selection of poems by Pilinszky, Hughes writes movingly about what he saw in the Hungarian writer, whose work, as he puts it, is both a mystery and a means of healing, a poetry that makes the imagery of the central mysteries of Catholicism and the imagery of the concentration camps 'become strangely interdependent'.[7] Hughes struggles to comprehend Pilinszky's Christianity, going to the heart of the struggle in the Hungarian writer's work between the will to go on believing in a God and the acknowledgement of the anguish and horror of the human condition after Auschwitz. Hughes questions the very nature of language for Pilinszky:

> It is impossible not to feel that the spirit of his poetry aspires to the most naked and helpless of all confrontations: a Christ-like posture of crucifixion. His silence is the silence of that moment on the cross, after the cry. In all that he writes, we hear a question: what speech is adequate for this moment, when the iron nails remain fixed in the wounds, with an eternal iron fixity, and neither hands nor feet can move? The silence of artistic integrity 'after Auschwitz' is a real thing.

Two things are evident from this introduction: firstly, that Hughes had an extraordinary empathy with Pilinszky, as with other Eastern European poets, notably Vasko Popa, which enabled him to read their poetry with a high degree of understanding, despite the language barrier. Secondly, it is clear that Hughes was, in a way, reaching out to other poets writing in other languages, making connections with his own search for poetry that could adequately express the contradictions of the world he inhabited. Hughes was a brilliant reader of other people's poetry and had the generosity to acknowledge the impact upon his own work of that of other poets, living and dead. Discussing the process of co-translating, he praises Csokits's drafts that 'retained naturally an unspoiled sense of the flavour and the tone of the originals ... the foreignness and strangeness.' What Hughes claims to have been aiming for was an English version that would not invent anything, but which would bring out the qualities that had attracted him to Pilinszky's poems in the first instance – 'their air of simple, helpless accuracy.'

The editorial introduction to the third issue of *MPT*, published in spring 1967 contains an explicit statement about Hughes's views of translation.[8] Noting that at that time there was a great deal of translation activity and plenty of translation theories, which are warmly welcomed, the editorial nevertheless takes a particular, strongly argued line:

> ... the first ideal is literalness, insofar as the original is what we are curious about. The very oddity and struggling dumbness of a word for word version is what makes our own imagination jump.[9]

Literal translation is thus seen as a way of establishing direct contact with the original author. The first hand contact, 'however fumbled and broken' is the authentic meeting. 'The minute we gloss his words', Hughes writes,' we have more or less what he said but we have lost him.' Once a translator takes over the words of another writer, the nature of the endeavour changes. By translating as literally as possible, by seeking to recreate the authentic sound of the original, the translator is reaching out to something 'alive and real' that has not been experienced before.

This theory of translation places great emphasis on the idea of translation as a search for something other, for different, unfamiliar voices. The translator who glosses the words of another writer is playing a kind of game, using what Hughes calls 'our own familiar abstractions', rather than reaching out to that which is different. However, there are two exceptions to this practice – where the translator is transformed and becomes an original poet through the process of translating, as in the case, Hughes suggests, of Arthur Whaley's translations from the Chinese, or where a translator is already so well established as a poet that 'we are glad to get more of him, extensions and explorations of his possibilities'. The example cited here is Robert Lowell's *Imitations* of Heine and Rilke. However, the editorial warns us that most translation remains on a much lower level:

> It pretends to be a parallel, or a recreation, which effectively misguides and deceives us in our attempt to re-imagine the original, and is of no interest in itself.

The idea of translation as a form of deceit is clearly stated here. The policy of the journal is uncompromisingly in favour of literalness as the only honest method of translating, though concessions are made to what are termed 'versions' and 'imitations':

> In this magazine, though we like to keep a steady bias, towards literalness and a true idea of our originals, as true a picture as possible of the poetry in other languages ,we would be delighted to print any kind of version or 'imitation' so long as it seemed to us inspired.

The intention is to reach all poets and all people who enjoy poetry, even though a secondary objective is to reach people with a genuine interest in foreign languages. The phrase 'a true idea of our originals' is a telling one, and Hughes's theory of translation is therefore based on a concept of ethics. Translation that is not literal becomes a traducement of the original, which then loses its veracity.

In an interview broadcast in 1982, Hughes talks again about how he worked on his translation of Seneca's *Oedipus*. He had some basic Latin, a Victorian translation and a word-for-word school crib. He began by reworking the literal translation, setting down variants of his own in brackets:

> Just plain stilted Latin sentences into an English vocabulary. A completely unreadable thing really. But that gave me the a sense of

what, maybe, there was in the original, which I couldn't get from the Victorian translation. All you got from that was stately Victorian-ness.[10]

Hughes argues that the Victorian translation concealed the original from him, hence the need to start from scratch and make his own literal version. Translation in this way becomes a sketch of an individual reading, but a reading that aspires to the authenticity of the original. In the case of Seneca, Hughes was working with actors who were performing his work even as he was translating it, and was also in dialogue with Peter Brook who similarly wanted to get to the essence of the play. Hughes explains that he kept stripping out the ornate elements of the language, until eventually he had reduced the text to barely 250 words. That process of reduction is depicted metaphorically as archaeological. Hughes talks about digging something out from the language of the original, discarding the ornateness of both Seneca's rhetoric and the elaborate Victorian crib and exposing what he refers to as 'the real core of the play.' In order to get to that core, he admits to having cut every mythological reference, which shortened the play by a third and then shortening every sentence. Through numerous drafts the process of cutting continued, until he finally ended up with 'a very short play...' a 'little naked knot'.

Translating Seneca was a prelude to the invented language of *Orghast*. Hughes at this stage was preoccupied with language, and in the same year he also wrote his important introduction to a selection of Shakespeare's verse. He was fascinated by what words could do, and yet also increasingly aware of the limitations of language. In an essay on *Orghast* that appeared in *Vogue* in 1971, he reflects on how at times fluency with words can mean less than half-formed speech. He describes conversations with two survivors of the Gallipoli campaign, one of whom spoke eloquently about his experiences, the other only in monosyllables. What perplexes him is that he found the more eloquent of the two less memorable:

> Both had lived through and registered the same terrific events. Yet words and natural, narrative, dramatic skill concealed everything in the one. While in the other, exclamations, hesitating vague words, I don't know what, just something about his half movements and very dumbness released a world of shocking force and vividness.[11]

Hughes's experience working with Peter Brook led him to further writing for the theatre, and in the last years of his life he produced several extraordinarily powerful versions of classic plays. In 1995 he finished translating Wedekind's *Spring Awakening*, that was performed later in the year at the Barbican, and wrote his version of Aeschylus' *Oresteia*. A year later, he translated Garcia Lorca's *Blood Wedding*, his version of Racine's *Phedre* came out in 1998, and in that same year he sent his version of Euripides' *Alcestis* to Barry Rutter at the Northern Broadside company. Both his versions of Ancient Greek tragedy were performed in 1999, the year after his death. If we take into account the fact that his *Tales from Ovid* appeared in 1997, this means that Hughes was translating compulsively, both poetry and drama for several years through the 1990s.

In his early statements about translation, Hughes made a clear distinction between literal versions and what he called imitations. His last work shows that this distinction still held, and the experience he had gained from working with actors also fed into his writing. *Alcestis* was performed by the Northern Broadside company, whose actors use Yorkshire pronunciation and sometimes also dialect to powerful effect. The fusion of colloquial-sounding speech with classical rhythms adds a new dimension to ancient tragedy.

The best way to see what Hughes does with the ancient Greek is to compare his version with that of another great translator, Richmond Lattimore, first published in 1955. Lattimore's version works well, is fluent and readable, but Hughes's version is much more physical and more explicitly contemporary. Hughes cuts out the children of Alcestis and Admetus, for example, focusing more on the relationship between husband and wife, reduces the role of the chorus and transforms the opening scene between Death and Apollo into a violent argument, Lattimore pits Death against Apollo in a ping-pong exchange between two equals, as this passage shows:

DEATH. My privilege means more to me when they die young.
APOLLO. If she dies old, she will have lavish burial.
DEATH. What you propose, Phoebus, is to favour the rich.
APOLLO. What is this? Have you unrecognised talents for Debate?
DEATH. Those who could afford a late death would buy it then.[12]

Hughes structures this scene quite differently. His Apollo is a far weaker figure than the powerful, domineering Death, though he pleads and tries to threaten. Death is given long speeches, and in the following he attacks Apollo for filling the minds of mankind with illusions of their own power, using colloquial language and transposing his argument into the modern world:

DEATH. As far as I am concerned, their birth-cry
  Is the first cry of the fatally injured.
  The rest is you – and your morphine.
  That is why they call you the god of healing.
  Life is your hospital and you call it a funfair.
  Your silly sickroom screen of giggling faces,
  Your quiverful of hypodermic syringes
  That you call arrows of inspiration.
  Man is deluded and his ludicrous gods
  Are his delusion. Death is death is death.[13]

*Alcestis* is a fascinating work, because though parts of it stay close to the original, elsewhere Hughes expands the play and introduces elements that are very much part of his own personal repertoire. Heracles in Hughes's version is given a long, very physical scene in which he acts out the story of his labours, which culminates in a vision he has of Prometheus on his crag. God appears on stage as a character, as does the vulture that tears out Prometheus's liver. Heracles shoots the vulture and frees Prometheus, who tells him the prophecy about God being deposed by his own son if he begets that son on the nymph Thetis. This, of course, is the story that gained Prometheus his freedom from torment.

At this point, the stage directions state that, 'Vulture reappears, reeking with smoke, feathers scorched to stumps, the arrow pulsing in her chest like a strobe light', and in a comic climax announces that it is not dead at all. Heracles shoots the vulture a second and third time, and the vision fades away. This lengthy, very visual scene offered the actors a chance for much greater physical action, since translating for the theatre for Hughes meant ensuring also that the actors could work to their strength. The relatively static quality of Ancient Greek tragedy is physicalized in Hughes's versions, ensuring a dramatic power that conforms to the norms of the contemporary theatre and matches the expectations of a contemporary audience.

The inclusion of the Prometheus scene also links *Alcestis* directly with Hughes's almost obsessive concern for this myth. But the great difference between this and earlier treatment of the Prometheus myth is in the way in which the story locks into the fundamental theme of the play, the triumph of life over death. Heracles becomes a central figure in Hughes's version, a grotesquely comic, yet ultimately heroic figure, a true friend to Admetus. He saves both Prometheus and Alcestis, wrestles with and defeats Death. Lattimore's version ends with a line spoken by the chorus stating that the story has come to an end, but Hughes's version ends with an affirmation: 'Let us give this man hope'. The final word, 'hope' resonates with unexpected power.

Hughes set aside his work on *Alcestis* for a time in 1995, to work on a version of the *Oresteia* which he rated very highly. This too is a very physical version, and here again Hughes infuses the text with a combination of contemporary language and powerful poetry. His is a very dramatic version, full of powerful visual images. In his translation of the chorus's account of the sacrifice of Iphigenia, the struggling girl is firmly located as a child of today's world, crying out to her father in simple English:

> The prayers go up. Her father
> Gives the signal. Iphigenia
> Is hoisted off her feet by attendants –
> They hold her over the improvised altar
> Like a struggling calf.
> The wind presses her long dress to her body
> And flutters the skirt, and tugs at her tangled hair –
> 'Daddy!' she screams. 'Daddy!' –
> Her voice is snatched away by the boom of the surf.[14]

Impossible not to recall one of Sylvia Plath's best-known poems, 'Daddy', with its terrifying portrayal of the father-daughter relationship in lines like:

> Every woman adores a Fascist,
> The boot in the face, the brute
> Brute heart of a brute like you[15]

The extraordinary power of Hughes's version can be seen clearly when compared to the translation of another great poet,

Robert Lowell's 1978 version. Lowell makes no attempt to introduce modern elements into the language or the story:

> 'Father, help me,' she cried, but her terror
> meant nothing to the kings in their impatience for
> the battle.
> Her father spoke the solemn prayers
> and ordered the priests to lift his child
> like a goat above the altar. Her robes
> fluttered like feathers, then she lay there fainting.[16]

The difference between Lowell's version and Hughes's highlights the eternal question facing translators: whether to take the reader back to the original, or whether to bring that original to the readers by providing them with elements that they can identify with and recognize. Hughes's theory of poetry translation is very much premised on the urge to send readers back to the original, but in the theatre he works quite differently, and all his translations are audience-focused. In his *Oresteia*, the plays are expanded to provide the audience with additional information that they may not have about the background to the horrors of the House of Atreus. Hughes skilfully weaves his additional material into the web of the translated sections, and the result is a highly accessible and performable version of the three plays that brings the audience into the underlying elements of the story right from the start.

What is also clear from the translations undertaken in the 1990s is that they fit into the development of Hughes's own writing rather than standing outside the rest of his output. For some writers, translation is a kind of added extra, a diversion from the linearity of the rest of their writing, but this is emphatically not the case with Hughes. Rather, his translations are logical next steps in his poetic career, taking up key themes that also appear in his other work. What is interesting is the extent to which writers from the ancient world spoke so importantly to him at that stage in his writing life that he chose to focus his efforts primarily on bringing them to a new generation of readers who were unfamiliar with Greek or Latin.

Though he had no reservations about including additional material in his play translations, Hughes's version of Ovid's *Metamorphoses* is deliberately entitled *Tales from Ovid*, indicating that this is not so much a translation, in Hughes's understanding of the term, but a sequence of poems inspired by Ovid, more of an imitation or, to use Pound's term, an homage. In his introduction, Hughes touches briefly upon the enduring power that Ovid's work exercised over centuries of readers in many different cultures, and then draws an explicit parallel between Ovid's age and his own. Ovid, he argues, was writing at a unique moment, when Christianity was emerging in the Roman Empire and the old religion was beginning to collapse, without anything new coming to take its place. The empire, he suggests, was

> at sea in hysteria and despair at one extreme wallowing in the bottomless appetites and sufferings of the gladiatorial arena, and at the other searching higher and higher for a spiritual transcendence – which eventually did take form, on the crucifix. The tension between these extremes, and occasionally their collision, can be felt in these tales. They establish a rough register of what it feels like to live in the psychological gulf that opens at the end of an era. And among everything else that we see, we certainly recognise this.[17]

There is an apocalyptic quality to this vision; Hughes compares the incipient collapse of the Roman Empire to his own world, pointing to what he terms the psychological gulf that opens up at the end of an era. Ancient writers were able to explore fundamental questions about the meaningfulness or mean- inglessness of human existence, and by producing his versions of some of those ancient texts, Hughes similarly explored existential questions for his own time. In the first section, when Jove is creating the universe, Hughes gives us a god pondering the value of his creation and musing on how to destroy his first attempt at human beings and make something better, since man has failed to live up to expectations:

> So now Jove set his mind to the deletion
> Of these living generations. He pondered
> Mass electrocution by lightning.
> But what if the atoms ignited,
> What if a single ladder of flame
> Rushing up through the elements
> Reduced heaven to an afterglow?[18]

Here the references to our own time are explicitly made: even Jove fears the prospect of a nuclear holocaust. The lightning bolts of the god could ignite the atoms in an explosion that might even destroy heaven, such is the potentially destructive power of what has been created.

This bleak vision reflects, as Hughes states in his introduction, a world in transition. But the primary focus of Ovid's *Metamorphoses* is what he terms 'hopelessly besotted and doomed love' that is transformed, metamorphosed, into something supernatural. Here we can see how Hughes's interest in shamanism connects with his reading of Ovid, how the shifting between worlds can lead to a process of transformation.

The final poem of *Tales from Ovid* is another story of doomed lovers, this time Pyramus and Thisbe, but though the poem , and the book, ends with their deaths, the final lines suggest a kind of hope, for the strength of love endures even beyond death:

> And the two lovers in their love-knot.
> One pile of inseparable ashes,
> Were closed in a single urn.[19]

Hughes was always acutely sensitive to opening and closing lines, and this final image is deliberately constructed to emphasize both the tragedy of death and the durability of love. Though burned to ashes, the lovers are together, inseparable now in the afterworld.

Hughes's last work is concerned with themes of restitution and redemption. Alcestis is restored to her husband, Orestes is pardoned and released from persecution by the Furies, the ashes of Pyramus and Thisbe are together for eternity. And while he was translating Greek and Latin works, he was also writing poems about his own inner process of restitution, about his relationship with his dead wife, Sylvia Plath. *Birthday Letters* astounded readers when it appeared in 1998 and aroused huge media attention. The collection brought the relationship between the two poets back into the public gaze, and invited a reassessment of the tragedy. Hughes had remained silent for so many years, and the breaking of the silence through poetry was therefore all the more powerful.

In her review, which is tinged with vestiges of the old feminist hostility to Hughes, Cora Kaplan points out that Hughes's lyric memoir invites readers to look again at Plath's own work, since it needs to be read alongside Plath's poems. She hails *Birthday Letters* as an unexpected gift, and notes that it 'plays endlessly on the reader's familiarity with Plath's mortal thoughts', adding that nevertheless

> It refuses to let the accreted scandal and tragedy of 'spilt lives congeal and stiffen to history' as Plath feared they might, trying instead for Ovid's poetic act of metamorphosis.[20]

Kaplan makes the connection between *Birthday Letters* and Ovid's *Metamorphoses,* an obvious link since Hughes was, for a time, working on both collections and a metamorphic process is apparent in both. There is, however, another connection, which is that both works have as their point of origin poems written by someone other than Hughes. In this respect, both works can be seen as a form of translation. With Ovid, Hughes translates the poems into the language of the twentieth century, stressing the theatricality of each individual story and creating some powerfully dramatic dialogue. With Plath, the process of translation is slightly different: there are echoes of her language in poem after poem, many of which consciously take up specific themes that she had developed. So, for example, Hughes's 'Child's Park' opens with a line that refers to Plath's poem about her dead father, 'Electra on Azalea Path', asking the question 'What did they mean to you, the azalea flowers?' Several poems have the same title as poems by Plath, such as 'Wuthering Heights', 'Totem' or 'Brasilia'. The poems engage with Plath's poems in a kind of dialogue, taking up keywords and images, sometimes offering alternative perspectives on an event or scene, as in 'You Hated Spain'. Hughes mentions this poem in an interview with Eilat Negev in 1996, in which he explains that having written a few poems, including this one, about his life with Plath, the effect on him was enormous and seemed to unlock something inside him.

*Birthday Letters* tells the story of the meeting between Hughes and Plath, traces their life together and the disintegration of their marriage, her development as a poet, the demons she could not escape from, her ultimate death and his subsequent life. The poems expose the fundamental differences between them: their different personalities, different histories, different cultural backgrounds, different expectations from life. A thread that runs right through the collection is the idea of miscommunication, of words spoken and misunderstood, a language apparently that they held in common but which neither could really comprehend. In 'Your Paris', he writes about decoding her words into a language that was entirely new to him, 'with conjectural, hopelessly wrong meanings'.

One of the most remarkable poems is 'Night-Ride on Ariel', that takes up the title of Plath's last collection. Hughes edited *Ariel* after her death, and resented criticism of his handling of his dead wife's manuscripts. 'Night-Ride on Ariel' pulls together several of Plath's primary images, such as the moon, electrocution, and the mother-figure, and names some of the women who had played an important role in Plath's life. The last section of the poem is full of words and phrases from some of Plath's last poetry: the line 'crackling and dragging their blacks' is a reference to the final line of 'Edge' – 'her blacks crackle and drag', while '...the last /Shred of the exploded dawn / In your fist –' takes up the final lines of 'Balloons', where the baby, their son Nicholas, bursts his balloon and is left with 'A red/Shred in his little fist'. Hughes 'translates' Plath in *Birthday Letters*, for as with any good translation, the reader is made aware of the existence of an original somewhere else. In this case, both the original and Hughes's version are accessible to the same readers, since both are written in the same language, and by reading the two sets of poems in counterpoint, the work of each poet acquires a different set of resonances. Hughes writes not to contradict Plath's version of events, but to offer his own alternative version.

In 1988 Hughes wrote a tribute to T.S. Eliot on the centenary of Eliot's birth, entitled 'The Poetic Self'. In this essay he uses translation as a metaphor to describe the huge shift from what he terms 'the God-centred metaphysical universe of the religions' to a universe that is 'psychological and centred on an idea of the self'.[21] This process described as translation has changed things for the poet, it has altered what he calls the climate and expectation of readers and it has altered the susceptibility of the poet to 'the trance condition' that is connected to the tradition of subjecting oneself to a greater authority. Hughes looks at Eliot's life, at his depression and other painful interior transformations that gradually changed him as a man and as a writer. In this essay, as in his other essays on the work of poets he admired, including Plath, Hughes shows his extraordinary sensitivity as a reader and exposes something of his own thought processes.

Back in the 1960s Hughes asserted that translation should never be a betrayal of an original, but should always seek to establish first-hand contact with the writer of that original. In his own work, that is what he consistently sought to do, whether the writer was his dead wife, or the composer of Ancient Greek tragedy. In an early version of his poem 'Untranslated', Weissbort reflects on Hughes's passion for translation, for projects completed, started or still in mind:

> ...and Aeschylus, the Oresteia –
> the Icelandic Sagas, an attempt at an appreciation –
> did you have in mind to embrace all this?
> And still more –
> There was Gilgamesh, for instance,
> Plans for a stage version?[22]

Hughes's translations dominate his final years and testify to his desire to understand more about the creative forces that drive poets to write at all times and in all cultures. One of his final poems, 'The Prophet', is subtitled 'After Pushkin'. Based on a literal version provided by Daniel Weissbort and Valentina Polukhina, who also provided notes and comments for him, it is an apocalyptic vision of the agonising transformation of a man into prophetic greatness. Split open by a knife-blade, his heart torn out and replaced with a flaming coal, his tongue torn out and replaced with a wise serpent's fork, the man lies on the stony ground like a corpse. Then, in the final lines, God calls him and commands him to go out into the world. The poet is God's instrument, God's interpreter:

> 'Stand, Prophet, you are my will.
> Be my witness. Go
> Through all seas and lands. With the Word
> Burn the hearts of the people.'

(*CP* 1194)

# Notes

## INTRODUCTION

1. Boyd Tonkin, 'The god of granite who could shatter stones with plain words', *The Independent*, 30 October 1998.
2. Edwin Muir, 'Kinds of Poetry', *New Statesman* vol. 54, 28 September 1957, 392.
3. Stephen Moss, 'Private Lines', *The Guardian*, 20 January 1998.
4. Karen V. Kukil, ed. *The Journals of Sylvia Plath 1950–1962* (London: Faber and Faber, 2000) 271.
5. Ted Hughes, 'Capturing Animals', *Poetry in the Making* (London: Faber and Faber, 1967) 15.
6. Seamus Heaney, 'Englands of the Mind' *Preoccupations. Selected Prose 1968–1978* (London: Faber and Faber, 1980) 151–2.
7. Daniel Weissbort, *Letters to Ted* (London: Anvil Press, 2002) 58.
8. Michael Parker, 'Hughes and the Poets of Eastern Europe' in Keith Sagar (ed.) *The Achievement of Ted Hughes* (Manchester: Manchester University Press, 1983), 51.
9. Ted Hughes: Language and Culture, Interview with Stan Correy and Robyn Ravlich, March 1982. http://ann.skea.com/ABC1.htm.
10. Ted Hughes, 'The Evolution of "Sheep in Fog"' in William Scammell (ed.), *Winter Pollen. Occasional Prose* (London: Faber and Faber, 1994), 191–209.

## CHAPTER 1. 'A SUDDEN SHARP STINK OF FOX': TED HUGHES AND NATURE

1. Interview with Ted Hughes, *The London Magazine*, January 1971, 11.
2. Seamus Heaney, 'Englands of the Mind', in *Preoccupations* (London: Faber and Faber, 1980), 154.
3. Ted Hughes *Poetry in the Making* (London: Faber and Faber, 1967), 15.

4. Ekbert Faas, *Ted Hughes: The Unaccomodated Universe* (Santa Barbara: Black Sparrow Press, 1980).

5. Ted Hughes, *Poetry in the Making* (London: Faber and Faber, 1967), 32.

6. Michael Parker, 'Hughes and the Poets of Eastern Europe' in Keith Sagar (ed.) *The Achievement of Ted Hughes* (Manchester: Manchester University Press, 1983), 45–6.

7. Ted Hughes, *Poetry in the Making* (London: Faber and Faber, 1967), 32.

8. Keith Sagar, *The Laughter of Foxes. A Study of Ted Hughes* (Liverpool: Liverpool University Press, 2000), 120.

9. Ted Hughes *Collected Poems* (London: Faber and Faber, 2003), 1204.

10. ibid. 1205.

11. ibid. 1211.

## CHAPTER 2. 'CROW LOOKED AT THE WORLD': THE POET AS SHAMAN

1. Martin Dodsworth, 'Ted Hughes and Geoffrey Hill', *The New Pelican Guide to English Literature* in Boris Ford (ed.) vol. 8 *The Present* (Harmondsworth: Penguin, 1983). See also Roy Fuller, 'Views', *The Listener* 11 March 1971, 297.

2. Stephen Coote, *The Penguin Short History of English Literature* (Harmondsworth: Penguin, 1993), 706.

3. 'Ted Hughes and Crow' in Ekbert Faas, *Ted Hughes: The Unaccommodated Universe* (Santa Barbara: Black Sparrow Press, 1980), 197-215. This and all subsequent citations are from this source.

4. Terry Gifford and Neil Roberts, *Ted Hughes: A Critical Study* (London and Boston: Faber and Faber, 1981).

5. Keith Sagar, *The Laughter of Foxes. A Study of Ted Hughes* (Liverpool: Liverpool University Press, 2000), 145.

6. Cited in Keith Sagar, 'The Story of Crow' in *The Laughter of Foxes*, 171–2.

7. *Crow*, Claddagh Records CCT 9–10, 1973. Cited in Keith Sagar, *The Art of Ted Hughes* (Cambridge: Cambridge University Press, 1975), 118.

8. 'Ted Hughes, Vasco Popa, 1967' in Ekbert Faas, *Ted Hughes: The Unaccommodated Universe* (Santa Barbara: Black Sparrow Press, 1980), 183–4.

## CHAPTER 3. 'BEING BRITISH IS A MYSTERY': HUGHES AND HIS ENGLISH ROOTS

1. Ted Hughes, *Collected Poems* (London: Faber and Faber, 2003), 1200.
2. ibid. 1200.
3. Keith Sagar, *The Laughter of Foxes. A Study of Ted Hughes* (Liverpool: Liverpool University Press, 2000), 152.
4. Thomas West, *Ted Hughes* ( London and New York: Methuen, 1985), 106.
5. Ted Hughes, *Collected Poems*, 1202.
6. Dennis Walder, *Ted Hughes* (Milton Keynes/Philadelphia: Open University Press, 1987), 28.
7. Keith Sagar, *The Laughter of Foxes. A Study of Ted Hughes* (Liverpool: Liverpool University Press, 2000), 31.
8. This and all subsequent quotations from the essay reprinted in Ted Hughes *Collected Poems*, 1219–22.
9. Diane Middlebrook, *Her Husband. Hughes and Plath – A Marriage* (New York: Viking, 2003), 257.

## CHAPTER 4. 'HIS VOICE FELT OUT OF THE WAY. "I AM", HE SAID': LANGUAGE AND MYTHOLOGY

1. Anthony Thwaite, 'Ted Hughes and Sylvia Plath' in *Poetry Today. A Critical Guide to British Poetry 1960–1995* (London: Longman, 1996), 54–62.
2. Robert Graves *The White Goddess* (London: Faber and Faber, 1961), 448.
3. ibid. 14.
4. Terry Gifford and Neil Roberts, *Ted Hughes: A Critical Study* (London and Boston: Faber and Faber, 1981), 19.
5. Keith Sagar, *The Laughter of Foxes. A Study of Ted Hughes* (Liverpool: Liverpool University Press, 2000).
6. Ted Hughes, *A Choice of Shakespeare's Verse* (London: Faber and Faber, 1971).
7. Ted Hughes, *Shakespeare and the Goddess of Complete Being* (London: Faber and Faber, 1992), 89.
8. Dennis Walder, *Ted Hughes* (Milton Keynes: Open University Press, 1987), 23.
9. Cited in A.C.H. Smith, *Orghast at Persepolis* (New York: Viking Press, 1972), 42.
10. Ted Hughes: *Language and Culture*, transcript of 'Doubletake' interview, 1982, transcribed by Ann Skea, *http://ann.skea.com/*

*ABC1.htm.* Subsequent quotations are from this same source.

11. Cited in A.C.H. Smith, *Orghast at Persepolis* (New York: Viking Press, 1972), 45.
12. ibid. 158–9.
13. Stuart Hirschberg, *Myth in the Poetry of Ted Hughes* (Dublin: Wolfhound Press, 1981), 134.
14. Keith Sagar, *The Laughter of Foxes. A Study of Ted Hughes* (Liverpool: Liverpool University Press, 2000), 168.


## CHAPTER 5. 'WITH THE WORD BURN THE HEARTS OF THE PEOPLE': TED HUGHES AND TRANSLATION

1. Seamus Heaney, 'Englands of the Mind', *Preoccupations. Selected Prose 1968-1978* (London: Faber and Faber, 1980), 156–7.
2. David Anthony Turner, 'A word about "Oedipus"' in Ted Hughes, *Seneca's Oedipus* (London: Faber and Faber, 1969).
3. Ekbert Faas, *Ted Hughes: The Unaccommodated Universe* Appendix II (Santa Barbara: Black Sparrow Press, 1980), 212.
4. Daniel Weissbort, 'Translation' in *Letters to Ted* (London: Anvil Press, 2002).
5. ibid. 96.
6. ibid. 96.
7. Introduction to *Selected Poems of János Pilinszky* (1976) in William Scammell (ed.) *Winter Pollen. Occasional Prose* (London: Faber and Faber, 1994), 229–36. All subsequent quotes are from this essay.
8. The editorial is unsigned, though it is written in the first person plural, purporting to be by both editors. Daniel Weissbort has assured me personally that Hughes wrote this and both men then agreed to let it go out as a joint statement.
9. Introduction, *MPT* 3 spring 1967, 1.
10. *Ted Hughes: Language and Culture*, transcript of 'Doubletake' interview, 1982, transcribed by Ann Skea, *http://ann.skea.com/ABC1.htm.*
11. Ted Hughes, *'Orghast*:Talking without Words' in *Winter Pollen* 122–7.
12. Richmond Lattimore, *Alcestis* in David Greene and Richmond Lattimore (eds.), *Euripides I* (Chicago and London: University of Chicago Press, 1955), 2–53.
13. Ted Hughes, *Alcestis* (London: Faber and Faber, 1999), 7.
14. Ted Hughes, *The Oresteia by Aeschylus* (London: Faber and Faber, 1999), 15.
15. Syliva Plath, 'Daddy', *Collected Poems* (London: Faber and Faber, 1981), 223.

16. Robert Lowell, *The Oresteia of Aeschylus* (London and Boston: Faber and Faber, 1978), 8.
17. Ted Hughes, *Tales from Ovid* (London: Faber and Faber, 1997), xi.
18. ibid. 21.
19. ibid. 254.
20. Cora Kaplan, 'Plath's Unquiet Slumbers', *The Times Higher Education Supplement* Feb. 27 1998, 25
21. Ted Hughes, 'The Poetic Self: A Centenary Tribute to T.S.Eliot' in *Winter Pollen*, 268–92.
22. Daniel Weissbort, *Eel Fishing, Poems to Ted* (Daniel Weissbort: Iowa City, 1999), 25.

# Select Bibliography

**WORKS BY TED HUGHES**

Unless otherwise indicated, Hughes's works are published by Faber and Faber, London and Harper and Row, New York.

*The Hawk in the Rain* 1957.
*Lupercal* 1960.
*Meet my Folks!* 1961 (US edn. Bobbs-Merrill, 1973).
*How the Whale Became* 1963 (US edn. Atheneum, 1964).
*The Earth-Owl and Other Moon People* 1963.
*Nessie the Mannerless Monster* 1964 (US edn. Bobbs-Merrill, 1974).
*Recklings* 1966 (Turret Press).
*Wodwo* 1967.
*Poetry in the Making* 1967 (US edn. *Poetry Is,* Doubleday, 1970).
*The Iron Man* 1968 (US edn. *The Iron Giant*).
*Seneca's Oedipus* 1969 (US edn. Doubleday, 1972).
*The Coming of the Kings* 1970 (US edn. *The Tigers' Bones,* Viking, 1974).
*Crow* 1970 (US edn. 1971).
*Eat Crow* 1971, radio play (Rainbow Press).
*Prometheus on his Crag* 1973 (Rainbow Press).
*János Pilinszky* 1976 (Manchester: Carcanet Press).
*Season Songs* (US edn. Viking, 1975; Faber 1976, 1985).
*Moon-Whales* (US edn. 1976; Faber 1988).
*Gaudete* 1977.
*Cave-Birds* 1978 (US edn. Viking, 1979).
*Moon-Bells* 1978 (London: Chatto).
*A Solstice* 1978 (Sceptre Press).
*Orts* 1978 (Rainbow Press).
*Adam and the Sacred Nine 1979* (Rainbow Press).
*Remains of Elmet* 1979.
*Moortown* 1979.
*Under the North Star* 1981 (US edn. Viking).

*River* 1983.
*What is the Truth?* 1984.
*Collected Animal Poems* (vol. 2) 1984.
*Flowers and Insects* 1986 (US edn. Knopf).
*Tales of the Early World* 1988 (US edn. Farrar and Strauss, 1991).
*Wolfwatching* 1989 (US edn. Farrar, Strauss and Giroux, 1991).
*Capriccio* 1990 (Gehenna Press).
*Shakespeare and the Goddess of Complete Being* 1992 (US edn. Farrar, Strauss and Giroux, 1992).
*Rain-Charm for the Duchy and Other Laureate Poems* 1992.
*The Iron Woman* 1993 (US edn. Dial Books, 1995).
*Three Books: Remains of Elmet, Cave-Birds, River* 1993.
*Winter Pollen* 1994 (US edn. Picador, 1995).
*New Selected Poems* 1995.
*The Dreamfighter* 1995.
*Difficulties of a Bridegroom* 1995 (US edn. Picador). Contains most of Hughes's short stories.
*Wedekind's Spring Awakening* 1995.
*Collected Animal Poems: The Iron Wolf, What is the Truth?, A March Calf, The Thought Fox* 1995.
*Lorca's Blood Wedding* 1996.
*Tales from Ovid* 1997 (US edn. Farrar, Strauss and Giroux).
*Birthday Letters* 1998 (US edn. Farrar, Strauss and Giroux).
*Racine's Phédre* 1998.
*The Oresteia of Aeschylus* 1999 (US edn Farrar, Strauss and Giroux).
*The Alcestis of Euripedes* 1999 (US edn. Farrar, Strauss and Giroux).
*Collected Poems* 2003.
*Letters of Ted Hughes*. Selected and ed. Christopher Reid 2007.

## OTHER WORKS

'Context' in *London Magazine* February 1962.
*The Poet Speaks (XVI): Ted Hughes Talks to Peter Orr* 1963 British Council.
'The Rock' in *Writers on Themselves* 1964 BBC 4.
Outline of *Orghast* in A.C.H. Smith, *Orghast* at Persepolis 1972 (London: Eyre Methuen).

## CRITICAL STUDIES

Bassnett, Susan, 'Plath Translated: Ted Hughes' *Birthday Letters*' in *Sylvia Plath: An Introduction to the Poetry* (London: Palgrave, 2005), 139–30.

Bell, Charlie, *Ted Hughes: A Beginner's Guide* (London: Hodder and Stoughton Education, 2002).

Bentley, Paul, *The Poetry of Ted Hughes: Language, Illusion and Beyond* (London: Longman, 1978).

Bishop, Nicholas, *Remaking Poetry:Ted Hughes and New Critical Psychology* (London: Harvester Wheatsheaf, 1991).

Churchwell, Sarah, 'Secrets and Lies: Plath, Privacy, Publication and Ted Hughes's *Birthday Letters' Contemporary Literature* 42.1: 2001, 102–48.

Dodsworth, Martin, 'Ted Hughes and Geoffrey Hill' *The New Pelican Guide to English Literature* Boris Ford (ed.) vol. 8. (Harmondsworth: Penguin, 1983).

Dyson, A.E., *Three Contemporary Poets: Thom Gunn, Ted Hughes and R.S.Thomas* (London: Macmillan, 1990).

Faas, Ekbert, *Ted Hughes:The Unaccommodated Universe* (Santa Barbara: Black Sparrow Press, 1980). This book contains useful interviews with Hughes and several of his prose pieces.

Feinstein, Elaine, *Ted Hughes. The Life of a Poet* (London: Weidenfeld and Nicolson, 2001).

Gammage, Nick (ed.), *The Epic Poise: A Celebration of Ted Hughes* (London: Faber and Faber, 1999).

Gifford, Terry and Neil Roberts, *Ted Hughes: A Critical Study* (London: Faber and Faber, 1981).

Heaney, Seamus, 'Englands of the Mind' *Preoccupations. Selected Prose 1968–1978* London: Faber and Faber, 1980), 156–7.

Hirschberg, Stuart, *Myth in the Poetry of Ted Hughes* (New York: Barnes and Noble, 1981).

Hobsbaum, Philip, 'Ted Hughes at Cambridge' *Dark Horse* no. 8, autumn, 1999, 6–12.

Middlebrook, Diane, *Her Husband. Hughes and Plath – A Marriage* (New York: Viking Press, 2003).

Myers, Lucas, *Crow Steered, Bergs Appeared* (Tennessee: Proctor Press, 2001).

Negev, Eilat, 'Ted Hughes Interviewed' *Daily Telegraph* 31 October 1999.

Robinson, Craig, *Ted Hughes as a Shepherd of Being* (London: Macmillan, 1989).

Sagar, Keith, *The Art of Ted Hughes* (Cambridge: Cambridge University Press, 1975), 2nd ed. 1978.

_____ *Ted Hughes* (Profile Books, 1981).

_____ (ed.), *The Achievement of Ted Hughes* (Manchester: Manchester University Press, 1983).

_____ (ed.), *The Challenge of Ted Hughes* (London: Macmillan, 1994).

_____ *The Laughter of Foxes* (Liverpool: Liverpool University Press, 2000).

Contains very useful bibliography and story of *Crow*.

Scigaj, Leonard M., The Poetry of Ted Hughes (University of Iowa Press, 1986).

Scigaj, Leonard M., *Ted Hughes* (Twayne, 1991).

Scigaj, Leonard M., *Critical Essays on Ted Hughes* (G.K.Hall, 1992).

Skea, Ann, *Ted Hughes. The Poetic Quest* (Australia: University of New England Press, 1994). A very useful website is *www.ann.skea.com*.

Uroff, Marjorie, *Sylvia Plath and Ted Hughes* (Urbana, Chicago and London: University of Illinois Press, 1979).

Walder, Dennis, *Ted Hughes* (Milton Keynes: Open University Press, 1987).

Warner, Erica, *Ariel's Gift: Ted Hughes, Sylvia Plath and the Story of Birthday Letters* (London: Faber and Faber, 2000).

Weissbort, Daniel, *Letters to Ted* (London: Anvil Press, 2002).

_____ (ed.), *Ted Hughes, Selected Translations, Poems* (London: Faber and Faber, 2006; New York: Farrar, Strauss and Giroux, 2007).

_____ *After Poems 1998* (London: Viper Press, 2008).

West, Thomas, *Ted Hughes* London, Methuen: 1985

# Index

Lightning Source UK Ltd.
Milton Keynes UK
UKOW052102311011

181250UK00001B/15/P